How To Enjoy Life and Not Feel Guilty

James L. Johnson

HARVEST HOUSE PUBLISHERS
Irvine, California 92714

HOW TO ENJOY LIFE AND NOT FEEL GUILTY

Copyright © 1980 by Harvest House Publishers
Irvine, California 92714

Library of Congress Catalog Card Number 79-85748
ISBN 0-89081-121-0

About the Author

James L. Johnson is the author of the *Code Name
Sebastian* series of novels, *What Every Woman
Should Know About a Man*, *Loneliness Is Not Forever*,
Profits, Power and Piety, and *Coming Back*.

He is an educator, journalist, former pastor, and
former missionary.

Contents

How To Enjoy Life and Not Feel Guilty

chapter one

Will the Real Guilt Please Stand Up?

SOMEONE once said, "When I come to the end of a perfect day, I check back carefully." The same sense of uneasiness occurs when a man or woman has gone any length of time without feeling guilty about something.

It is not difficult to feel guilty if we think long enough about the world, the suffering in it, and the sense of personal affluence versus those with nothing. We can feel guilty about self-image, whether we have done right by our children, or whether we are doing right by God. We can check over any given day if we wish to do so and find times here and there when perhaps something better could have been said, something wiser, or something done with greater effect, and perhaps that is true.

And many people do just that. It seems that so much of a person's life is spent either running from a past sin or thinking there is one lurking around the corner. It also seems that man is forever building new defenses against it—rationalization, indifference, and a kind of self-narcotizing. Between becoming a victim of it and trying to defend against it is enough to exhaust any soul—and there are many who have cracked physically or mentally under this pressure. There really is no way to avoid it and there is no way to defend against it unless the individual pulls it all together under a loving God and stops the continual fixation on it.

THE ANXIOUS CHRISTIANS

Though the Bible says "Be not anxious for your life" (Matthew 6:25 ASV), the Christian, like others on society's treadmill of the anxiety prone, can often feel that sense of someone gaining on him or her. Christ's promise, "Peace I leave with you; not as the world giveth . . . . Let not your heart be troubled or afraid" (John 14:27), somehow gets lost in the smoking circuits of an overanxious soul. "If we confess our sins, He is faithful and just to forgive us our sins . . ." (1 John 1:9) is a promise, but guilt goes on nevertheless.

This matter of guilt, no matter how the most saintly of people seek to deal with it or ignore it, pops out like measles one day and a rash the next day. It shows in the striving on the one hand to be very rigid morally in order to avoid any twinge of guilt, or else it shows up on the other hand in the man or woman who deliberately attempts to live a free-wheeling lifestyle, desperately hoping to cut loose and do all and everything, trying to convince himself or herself that there is really nothing bad enough to feel guilty about. Both attempts are wrong, unhealthy, and unspiritual.

The whole problem with guilt is that it can *harm*, as James Dolby said in his book *I Too Am Man*: "Guilt feelings can harm and possibly destroy the dynamic personality structure. A man can bend and break under the consequences of a violated conscience."[1]

RIGHT AND WRONG GUILT

Let it be said at the outset that guilt is a safety valve. It is not something to be dismissed or rationalized out of existence. If man did not have a sense of guilt when he violated the codes of law in a society, there would be only chaos. If man did not have a sense of value on which to base his actions, then his responsibility to man would die. Guilt is a means of helping correct an individual's course for self and others.

We must realize that there is a *rightful guilt* and a *wrongful and harmful guilt*. As John McKenzie put it in his book *Guilt: The Meaning and Significance,* "Guilt is based upon something that the person feels he ought to have done and didn't. When he or she feels something 'ought to be' has not, then it will come; and if there is responsibility for not doing the 'ought,' it becomes deep-seated."₂ The Christian knows about the "oughts" from Scripture, and he knows when the "ought" has been allowed to slip.

However, given the legitimate place of guilt in a person's life, it still comes down to *who* is defining it. That is the problem this book seeks to deal with. True, there is a level of distinctive lifestyle for the Christian that is Biblically based, but there is also the matter of trying to live a lifestyle that is purely *man-based.* When a person tries to live according to someone else's private view of sin and morality, then problems occur. What comes then is the harmful, unnecessary guilt patterns. This guilt is not the "ought-to-have-done-and-didn't" kind. This is the guilt spawned by "I-think-he-or-she-felt-I-ought-to-and-I-didn't." *That is a big difference.*

When the individual takes on someone else's interpretation of what is right or wrong, this creates a wrong and harmful anxiety-guilt pattern. The church often gets trapped into this kind of role, because as a spiritual authority image in the Body, it (or its representatives) may feel that it is the ultimate custodian of other people's lives, including their morality.

Joe, for instance, and his son ate Sunday dinner and went out in the backyard to toss a Frisbee. They were having a good time until Charlie B., the neighbor next door and head elder of Joe's church, came out and sat down on a lawn chair. No Frisbee for him! No activity at all. That was his privilege. But for Joe, he suddenly felt a twinge of guilt—his elder seemed to be "observing the Sabbath" properly. No work, no activity, period. Joe and his son, however, seemed to be violating that. So activity on Sunday suddenly became a point of tension. Perhaps Charlie wasn't thinking anything at all about Joe and his son playing Frisbee. But for Joe, he suddenly felt he was less spiritual than Charlie and began to feel guilt.

The Frisbee-tossing ended. Joe took his son inside and played Monopoly with him instead.

It was not enough that "the Sabbath was made for man and not man for the Sabbath" (Mark 2:27); instead, one man's activity, his own choice for Sunday, seemed to form a judgment on the other person. Whether intended or not (or expressed or not), the result was unnecessary anxiety and guilt for Joe. Somehow in Joe's mind Charlie was the spiritual authority figure—what he did on Sunday everyone should do.

But man is forever making rules for himself, drawing a great many rules from those who are older, stronger (perhaps), more authoritarian, or more spiritual. From childhood every person learns to draw on the rules learned in the household and the schoolroom. Everyone has created a level of a value system based on an authority structure in the past.

THE BIBLE AS A BOOK OF LIFE

However, the Bible is not a book of rules. It lists behavioral principles mostly. The Bible does not persistently define morality in every given situation. It does provide a broad plain of ethics, values, and morality that a man can interpret and apply to himself in cooperation with the Spirit of God within him. God stayed away from listing specific rules in every case, perhaps because He knew that some of those rules would alter later with culture change.

Of course, there are some areas that are categorical: "Be angry, and sin not" (Ephesians 4:26); "Come apart and be separated" (2 Corinthians 6:17); "Thou shalt not steal" (Matthew 19:18). Others, including the Sermon on the Mount, are clear enough. And believers take from these some sense of value to form a distinctive lifestyle that is pleasing to God.

When the Bible is taken only as a book of *rules* and not a book of *life*, a person can't help but feel guilt and anxiety constantly. As much as Paul warned that "all things are lawful but not all things are expedient [advantageous]" (1 Corinthians 6:12), too many believers take a position of judgment on the word "expediency" and avoid the words "all things are lawful." What Paul is saying is that there is nothing in itself that is to be considered "unlawful" in terms of indulgence. But in the same light he also says that every Christian should ask, "Will it do me any good, build me up, help me be a better Christian and maybe help someone else too?" *But no one else can make that judgment for him.*

So then the Bible, if looked on as a book of rules instead of a book of life, soon begins to shrink the soul of the believer to the size of a pea. One cannot continually squeeze the chamber of the inner spiritual being without its finally dying. Push a child to extreme conformity to the laws of a household and sooner or later he will find ways to break that law just to establish independence. Or else he will become incapable of feeling any sense of freedom in the constriction of it all. Love never pushes to extremes. The Bible is love, not law. God trusts His own to know the territory they are in and to act accordingly. But when any individual allows others to interpret the right and wrong of a lifestyle, even out of the Bible, that is a wrong imposition that God never intended.

No man or woman can live forever as a healthy Christian looking over his or her shoulder, afraid of being "caught" at something that is supposed to fit *someone else's* standards of what is Biblically right or wrong. If one is confused, he or she should seek counsel. But until then each person must find his or her own way in partnership with God Himself.

THE FEAR OF MAN

One woman who had to have dinner adjoining a bar in the same room suddenly caught sight of another member of her church. In the middle of her soup she bolted from the table. "Oh, God, don't let her see me here!" she moaned as she fled, leaving her astounded partners in a state of confusion. The presence of a bar in the same room, though none at her table were imbibing, was perfectly okay until someone else showed up.

"The fear of man is a snare" (Proverbs 29:25) is a truth too often experienced by too many people. Many Christians live their lives in terms of fear of man rather than of God. Though God "condemns not," it is man who seems to have the superior hand. "Judge not that you be not judged" (Luke 6:37) is Biblical, but few people are willing to stand by this principle in light of circumstances that may appear marginal in the moral code of someone else.

One man became so consumed with guilt about his "lustful thoughts" that he could not do a decent day's work in the office. He kept his head down, eyes closed in prayer, mumbling prayers about "my awful sinfulness." He never looked to the right or left. He never looked up at a woman who might address him in the course of the business day. He scooted in to his desk in the morning and skittered out at night. His morbid introspection literally destroyed him. When asked if he thought God was giving him conviction about lust, he seemed confused. In other words, guilt was not from God; it was born out of a fear of his soul catching his mind thinking impure thoughts. Beyond that it was a fear that someone might "catch him" looking at a woman directly and conclude that he had lustful thoughts for her.

His history from childhood had been filled with the brand of Biblical law that became a policeman to him rather than a loving statement of care and concern. Sex was drilled into him as something ugly that would ultimately destroy him if he indulged in one single thought of it. "Someone will always find you out if you play with sex," his father warned. Thus was born a spiritual cripple from five years of age. The end of that man was a nervous collapse. Fortunately he came out of it through careful therapy and a return to the "law of love."

Anxiety and guilt kills, but a wrong conception of internal guilt is even worse because it is a *self-inflicted* thing and not of God. It kills not just the green shoots of creativity and personality and the feeling of a caring God, but it also kills internally. Tension out of guilt plays havoc with the heart and intestines.

As Leslie Weatherhead, pioneer in the field of pastoral psychology, put it, "In all psychotherapeutic practice it is found that the sense of guilt plays a large part. Sometimes, indeed, guilt, either conscious or repressed, is a determining factor in neurosis . . . and responsible for the onset of serious physical symptoms."[3]

But why take on more guilt than is necessary? Why take on someone else's judgment or code of morality? This is the tragedy of too many lives. When the individual has violated a specific territory of God's expected character, then let guilt have its way of rectifying it. "Sin" is what the person senses by the Spirit of God within, and the resolving of that is to make it right with Him, and where necessary to make it right with the one offended.

THE UNHAPPY AND HAPPY CHRISTIAN

The unhappy Christian is the one who has allowed others to determine for him how he should act, behave, and respond in life—what he can eat, drink, see, or enjoy. Those who allow this are constantly afraid of the judgment of others. They are afraid to be themselves lest what they are may become an object of judgment by others. This is what John Powell meant in his book *Why Am I Afraid to Tell You Who I Am?* "But, if I tell you who I am, you may not like who I am, and it is all that I have."[4] Or again, "If I expose my nakedness as a person to you—do not make me feel shame."[5]

Jesus came to "give life and that more abundantly" (John 10:10), but few can find it or live it if they are constantly under the cloud of guilt. Abundant life is not spawned by fear. Jesus did not come to add to the weight of man but to deliver him from that weight. On the one hand the sin that entered the universe in the Garden of Eden has been lifted by redemption, but on the other hand it is God's desire that this same person know freedom from guilt constantly. Otherwise the blood is not sufficient.

None of this suggests that the Christian should live his life unto himself or herself. Every believer seeks to *glorify* God in his newfound redemption. Anyone who seeks less than this will not be happy either. The believer is supposed to be relaxed between what he or she knows is pleasing to God (not always to other people) and what is a normal, natural way of life which God is not particularly anxious about. To know the difference and the extent of the difference is surely within the heart of the believer. *It cannot be left to someone else to decide.* It is not God acting then, but man. And then it becomes a human code and not a code of God.

THE CHRISTIAN CHARADES

And yet the peculiar charades go on. Christians—not all, but too many—continue to pick their way through life, bobbing and weaving around the Pharisaical presence.

"Duck!" the man at the table warned. All four heads went down. What happened? The local "priest" had just come in, and with him the "presence of the sacred law." What were the five doing? Playing cards. Is that something old hat? No. At least not to the five whose initial reaction indicated it was not.

A Jewish man from a kibbutz in Israel wanted to honor three Christian young men for their help in one of his special projects during the year. He knew no other way than to order wine for a simple toast. The three, not wishing to offend, accepted his gesture. As they lifted their glasses to his, their pastor walked in. All three dropped their glasses, and the Jewish man had to face them only with his own glass lifted. The honor bestowed became an insult, but the three were at least not "caught."

It may be true that there is a greater sense of moral laxity on the part of the church regarding Christian lifestyle these days. It may be that there needs to be more careful teaching on what is true morality and value. It may be that there is more Christian divorce and deviant sexual behavior, more dishonesty and "winebibbing." But the question is: Has this occurred because of the lack of more rules or because there is now forming a kickback at those who would dictate *practice* rather than Biblical *principles?* Are people just now awakening to the fact that they are not little children, that they can glorify God without someone reading the law to them? Could it be that believers are only now beginning to sense that they and God— *they and God*—are in a compact together, and *not* they and the church, or they and other believers?

LET GUILT COME FROM GOD

There is a time to feel guilt, yes. But let it come from God.

The woman taken in adultery stood in shame before her accusers (John 8:3-7). She had been caught in the act. But Jesus had compassion for this one who had been dragged before Him by her peers and superiors. He knew the body. He knew what was there. According to the law He could have condemned her, as the others did. Instead, He said, "Neither do I condemn thee; go and sin no more" (John 8:11).

Was Jesus condoning adultery? No. But He was reminding this woman that even in the sin she had committed (which others had judged by the law) He was not judging her. Love took the place of law. There are many who are "caught" by fellow believers who gain no such reprieve, even for the "lesser sins." This is what destroys the life of God.

Paul Tournier in his book *Guilt and Grace* differentiates between mature and immature guilt like this: "For true guilt is precisely the failure to dare to be oneself. It is the fear of other people's judgment that prevents us from being ourselves, from showing ourselves as we really are, from showing our tastes, our desires, our convictions, from developing ourselves and from expanding freely according to our own natures."[6]

In Psalm 51 David asked for God's forgiveness. With that came inner peace. There is a time to make things right, but God is the quickest of all to accept that attempt and provide release from it. But when one must live in the nightmare of wondering if it is necessary to continue to take on false guilt of another person's making, then that life has lost touch with the reality of God. For it is He and He alone who judges in the end.

One cannot go through life completely free of guilt. But one can certainly know the Source of forgiveness and use it. At the same time it is essential to know what is the conviction of God and what is the judgment of peers.

chapter two

The Guilt of
Not Fitting In

CONFORMITY. "Look, just fit in, do what the others do, don't do anything out of the ordinary, and you'll do just fine." This was a wife's advice to a husband who had not been a Christian very long and was facing a social gathering of Christians. In other words, "Don't do anything that is unpredictable."

The man, of course, was unpredictable. That was his lifestyle. He enjoyed it. He would wiggle his ears while conversing, or light a match while conversing, or pull an egg out of his pocket, because his days of being a magician were not yet gone. He enjoyed being unpredictable, and he always thought others did too.

But now he had to "fit in." This was a very "sedate, careful, circumspect social gathering." There would be prayer and maybe some Bible reading. "Don't rock the boat." So the man went and played the game. He pulled no tricks, told no jokes, was as polite as a diplomat in conversation, and tried to keep from yawning. When it was over, he drove home in silence. He had conformed, but now he was confused. He was not himself anymore. He belonged to other people's expectations of him as that of a "Bible-believing, born-again Christian"—which to him meant three hours of a boring, uneventful, joyless social.

In his book *Do I Have to Be Me?* Lloyd Ahlem stated, "In nonauthentic living, there is a behavioral recipe to follow in nearly every social situation. If we know the place where we are going to be and the kind of people who will be there, our

behavior can be predicted fairly well. We will un-
consciously follow the behavioral recipe that fits
the situation.",

There are times when it is necessary to do just
that. Nobody wants to deliberately jar the delicate
bubble that encases the finery of the kingdom.
There are times when occasions call for the
sublimating of personal lifestyle to the parameters
of others.

But how long does one do that and maintain personal identity? Is God's kingdom made up of
punch-press figures, all with the same design, all
with the same lines, all with the same polite decor?
Does one forever play the game? Does one forever
take on the nuance that someone else has
developed? Does one forever put aside the "me" in
order to be accepted by "them"?

No, playing the game inevitably destroys a major part of the self that God has given to the individual. Yet if a man tries to be himself, he soon
feels guilty. Someone will ultimately communicate
to him that "this is simply not done." At that point
this person can abandon the Christian culture and
be himself, or else the Christian culture can say to
him, "Come, be yourself, and share what you are."
Which is it to be?

THE LANGUAGE GAME

Language. The right language. Ah, yes!
Language is the first conformity level. It must be
nonoffensive and "in the Spirit." It must be lyrical.
It must roll with the rushing surf of dogmatism. It
must "sound" Christian.

"It is my prayer that the poor people of Cambodia . . ." etc., etc.

"The Aristotelian concept of the universe won't fit the Augustinian theory of life which is to be lived . . ." etc., etc.

"I praise the Lord that . . ." etc., etc.

"As for Niebuhr in his theological approach to the matter of force in righting the world's wrongs . . ." etc., etc.

"It was a glorious testimony . . . a prostitute . . . can you believe? And now a Christian . . ." etc., etc.

"I'M HUNGRY!"

Silence. Somebody goofed. It just does not fit the language of the hour. Hungry? What has that to do with Aristotle, Augustine, Niebuhr, or that glorious testimony? Or even the Cambodians? Yes, it comes close to the Cambodians. But did anybody catch it? No. Who is this buffoon who dares to declare his physical appetite in the midst of the "higher levels" of language exchange?

Harry. Harry who? "My word! Did he say he was hungry?"

Harry was not predictable, obviously. And poor Harry, though fed, went home with indigestion. Some folks just can't speak the language. Or won't. All they know is the language that expresses need. Hunger? Loneliness? The need to talk about plumbing? Mechanics? Algebra? But there is no room for that. Oh, yes, there are times, and not all Christians come under the sweeping indictment. But who hasn't stood in a room listening to the "saintly language" and not felt like an outsider?

How does one conform to language? Some don't know it. Some can't speak it. And since they cannot, they feel guilty, alone, pushed aside, unwanted—whether or not that was intended. Harry goes home feeling anxious. His wife will make him feel anxious if he does not. In the night anxiety will wake him up. He committed a "no-no."

As Ahlem put it, "While playing predictable roles gives us certainty about each other, it can stereotype the uniqueness right out of us. Our freedom to act spontaneously and honestly gets lost. Further, we force ourselves into molds that often fit us uncomfortably in an attempt to absolve conflict between the mold and our true selves. More and more of our behavior becomes patterned uncomfortably after some expected role. To reduce conscious stress, we subdue our sensitivities and our true feelings . . . ."[2]

Is it any wonder that a non-Christian in such a gathering is totally baffled, lonely, and bored? Is it any wonder that he or she feels more guilty and outof it?

But Harry, a Christian of three years? Yes! Language can make or break.

The Conformity Game

Who has not sat at a dinner table listening to the major figure of the evening espousing on the significance of the number seven in Deuteronomy without feeling guilty? "I can't even find Deuteronomy!"

So guilt. Then anxiety. "I better find Deuteronomy!" Or, "Why don't I know about that number seven in Deuteronomy?" So the language is not there. Conformity to the accepted phrases, lines, and Biblical passages is necessary to make the mileage in the social gathering. But is it? Thank God for hostesses who catch it quickly, and who politely and delicately sense that not *everyone* around that table is so astute Biblically or theologically. "Harry, I understand you are doing a major plumbing job for the school." And Harry is saved! Saved from guilt, saved from anxiety, because he does not have the language, yet someone is inviting him to say his thing his way.

"You became a Christian how?"

"Well . . . I was driving down this expressway and saw this billboard that said, 'I have come to give you life and that more abundantly.'"

"And you became a Christian on that?"

"Well . . . I went home and asked my wife what she thought. And I said I think that's the answer—"

"You did it by yourself?"

"Pardon?"

"You saw a billboard sign and became a Christian?"

"Yes . . . well, I know it's a bit strange . . . ."

"It's not done! Surely someone counseled you! Surely you sought out someone?"

"Well . . . I talked to God—"

"You—what? Just like that? Nobody else? Don't you understand you need someone skilled to explain the way of salvation? Now, look . . . there is the process of regeneration whereby the Spirit moves in and transforms the old man into the new. You must first pray the prayer of a sinner. Then you must accept Him into your life. You just don't do that by yourself! Someone must lead you, pray with you. There must be a confirmation of the Spirit that you are in the faith! I mean, you must give public witness to your conversion, you must stand before all and confess you are a sinner and *then* you know the glorious transformation, all right?"

"Oh . . . well, maybe I—I didn't read the sign right after all . . . sorry about that."

The first step in pushing aside any guilt about language is to accept the other's language while communicating one's own. It may not be theologically sweet or philosophically a bowler ball, but it is what constitutes the person.

"Have you caught the ontological, cosmological, metaphysical aspects of the Pauline Epistles?"

"No, but I know the Lord gave me a job today."

The scholar can speak his language and the plumber his. The professor speaks his own and the carpenter his own. The conductor of the symphony speaks his and the bagger at the supermarket speaks his. That is the beauty and the wonder and the glory of the Body! The head of the board of education speaks her line, but the housewife who has had a full day of changing diapers speak her own! There should never be anxiety over the lack of speaking someone else's very "erudite" language.

The only way to prevent the guilt of conformity in language is to refuse to feel cowed by someone else's dominance with the "saintly language." Saintly language is all right, but not everyone speaks it exactly the same way or in the same context. "God is good" makes as much sense as "The everlasting providence of God, the surfeiting of the paucity of our souls, the manifestation of the angelic hosts, the super-inundating presence of the Holy Spirit, the sublime Paraclete . . . to Him forever, Amen!" (Or does one make sense to all, and the other only to the speaker?)

THE GREETING GAME

But there is also conformity in lifestyle. Italians kiss the girls goodbye; Swedes shake hands; the Dutch smile. The believer who kisses a friend who is going away is out of sync, though the kiss is holy in every sense and is the only proper gesture to express appreciation and at the same time loss. Some will hug in their joy; some will remain very rigid in comportment; some will just weep tears.

There is an intimacy in the Body that is seldom expressed. Everyone has the right to his own choice of expression, of course. But it is strange that believers, who are so bound in the mystery of the union with God, remain so aloof from each other and cannot tolerate the articulation of affection. So it is that human relationships in the Body remain within the bounds of affectionless and expressionless love.

But apart from that (for there is no way it will change), sometimes people feel guilt if they express affection in all sincerity toward another person. The style is simply not to do so. Yet something is missing when it is not, for in the holiness of this kind of communion there is the heightened sense of the value which one person places on the other.

One man of 53 kissed his secretary of 12 years goodbye because he felt so moved in how much she had meant to him in their work relationships. The secretary took it coolly, and simply gave him her hand as a warning that a kiss was not her way of saying goodbye. So be it. Though she was 32 years old and he was 21 years her senior, to her it was "out of line." To that man it was the highest form of compliment, yet he went home guilty because he sensed he had done her wrong.

Perhaps the reason there is so little true warmth in the fellowship today is that too many in the Body remain so aloof from each other. Whether or not it is a kiss is not the issue. There seems to be a barrier between people, a refusal to express, a nervousness about corporateness, an antsiness about a touch and a hug. To interpret such gestures as sexual is to demean the intent. There is a difference, and to judge a kiss as anything but pure (apart from a true basis for the judgment) is to create unnecessary anxiety in the other person.

So the acceptable level of Christian relationships never goes very deep. Conformity to stiff, sterile, polite communication, especially for those who weep, for those who bid farewell, or for those who have given so much of life and work and dedication to another person, is to impose an unreal level of true spirituality. By no means should everyone "greet each other with a holy kiss" on Sunday morning, lest the congregation never get settled down to serious worship. But there is a time to do just that—either to greet or to say goodbye. There should be no guilt in the purity of that. How does the world conclude "see how they love one another" unless there is some genuine affection that is bound up in the love of Christ and some demonstration of it within the bounds of discretion?

CAN GOD ENJOY LAUGHTER?

Lifestyle is not a straight line for the Christian. Everyone differs in expression and the form of their communication. What about laughter? Joy? God is not a gray, overcast sky. Laughter is laughter. Hard or soft, it is laughter, but it needs to be expressed in the fullness of what the individual's own personality allows.

One man who had spent four hours at a social one evening remarked to his wife before they fell asleep, "I didn't hear one genuine laugh all night. Were the jokes all that bad? Or is it that laughter is a kind of mockery of God?"

Christians seem to be humorless. Not all, thank God. But when a man who likes to laugh gets into a group that takes life too seriously and won't laugh, that man may feel guilty if he lets out with a guffaw. People look at him in some wonder, as if laughter was not given to man in redemption, but only the burden of the cross and the darkness of death. Resurrection is laughter—not joking laughter, but laughter. It is the joy of the laugh that says death has lost and life has won!

The woman who scolded her seven-year-old in church for giggling about something he was reading in the Sunday school paper said, "God doesn't like laughter in church!" The boy never forgot it. He never laughed again in any spiritual setting. From then on, his life in God was severe in countenance. He always appeared unhappy and died eventually as a man who "laughed little, but perhaps he had it inside."

CONFORMITY TO CHRIST

Lifestyle always comes down to movies, plays, cards, wine, or whatever list will suit to make the proper distinctions from non-Christians. Conformity to these can be burdensome. God alone gives life, and each individual must dress himself or herself in what He gives. It is God who mixes people and personalities, and therefore there will be varieties of styles. That in no way opens the door to license to do anything and everything. Lifestyle is what God gives to each person, so therefore those styles will be different.

The key is *conformity to Christ* and not conformity to man. It is the same old principle: Conformity to man negates the individual identity of a person, presses him into another person's mold, and forces him to act, respond, and react in exactly the same way. If anything seems to be out of joint, guilt sets in. Many a woman has become flustered and anxious over the fact that her style of dress was not the function of the hour. Many a man has fussed over the fact that his choice of jokes was not in keeping with the group. People worry about their images, wondering if they are coming off in terms of the models set for them by those more successful, or those who seem to be the judges of what is right and wrong in lifestyle.

The "conformity-to-Christ" principle is to continually move to His image. That image is not drab, withdrawn, overpious, or one-dimensional. It is His character that is taken on, but that does not negate the individual's personality. Both the extrovert and the introvert are to be what they are while becoming more like Christ. This does not mean withdrawal or denial of self as much as it does taking on the positive attributes of His love, compassion, and commitment.

This refusal to give up personality in terms of conformity to other personalities is to preserve the precious uniqueness of the individual whom God made in the first place. Authentic people refuse to be molded by anyone but God. Each person is shaped by what he sees in others and what he sees in God. But to grow is to take from both of these the attributes that are worthy, that build, that structure.

PERSONAL UNIQUENESS

Conformity to other people's lifestyles is to deny personal uniqueness in God. Only the individual knows what are the bounds, what is right and wrong before God. To be conformist is to cancel creative genius within, the wealth of distinct gifts to be shared, the uniqueness of the self that must be shared in order for others to be enriched.

But then why do people continually try to conform to everyone else's levels of life, uniqueness, judgments, or behavior? It comes down to a problem of self-image. People who conform are mostly afraid that what they are is not quite good enough for "them." There are success images which the

Christian crosses every day; the success images are those who are looked to as having some specific level of attainment, either morally or otherwise.

This was the tragedy surrounding one young man who committed suicide at a Christian college. In the course of his study he felt he was not rising to the standards of the "successful ones" around him. To say he was wrong to judge himself in terms of others has to take into consideration the fact that his Christian culture somewhere communicated that to him, in the first place. Attempts to conform are usually attempts to find acceptance, to relieve the guilt about not being accepted. Those who insist on conformity to whatever it may be are in fact forcing others to be other than themselves. They become unreal, not authentic, dishonest with themselves, conscious of being dangled on the end of a string, like a puppet.

Lloyd Ahlem again states, "We struggle to see ourselves in essentially positive ways. If distortion of self-image is necessary, we resort to it. We prize our self-perceptions and psychological integrity more than our sanity. When the human mind perceives too much threat, it will resort to psychotic symptoms if necessary. Mental illness is best thought of as the most efficient available means of preserving integrity."[3]

There is a point when one can become so religious in order to conform that no one can put up with it. It is unreal, it is dishonest, and it communicates a sense of heavy-handed judgment.

Again Ahlem put it right when he said, "People who have little need to protect themselves psychologically [or spiritually] lead the most enjoyable lives. They are free to experience relationships fully and free to be empathetic to need. They spend little energy maintaining arsenals of automatic responses to perceived threats."[4]

Guilt that emerges from lack of conformity to others is the worst of all forms. Guilt can only be handled by forgiveness or punishment. But further, it can be handled if the individual traces it to the fact that it comes from trying to be someone else. God does not give guilt for accepting self as His own creation. Therefore being honest and accepting of the self is a compliment to God. To negate self is to literally say to Him, "You have made me wrong. I can't be what I am, and I can't be what he or she is, no matter how I try." In the end, that person withdraws into a shell or else becomes emotionally and spiritually ill.

THE FREEDOM OF GOD AT WORK

Playing the game in order to be accepted, to conform in order to be approved, is a poor defense mechanism. It is not the freedom of God at work.

Paul wrote, in Romans 12:2-5, "Don't copy [or be conformed to] the behavior and customs of this world, but be a new and different person, with fresh newness in all you do and think. Then you will learn from your own experience how his ways will really satisfy you. As God's messenger I give each of you God's warning: Be honest in your estimate of yourselves, measuring your value by how much faith God has given you. Just as there are many parts to our bodies, so it is with Christ's body. We are all parts of it, and it takes every one of us to make it complete, for we each have different work to do. We belong to each other, and each needs all the others" (The Living Bible).

Rabbi Zusya put it this way:

In the world to come I will not be asked, "Why were you not Moses?" I shall be asked, "Why were you not Zusya?"

This is the point. Trying to be Moses when we are not brings guilt in not attaining to be a Moses. "I am all I got" is enough. To perfect oneself is perfectly legitimate; it is *not* legitimate when one seeks to perfect oneself in the image of someone else.

chapter three

Who Judges?

IT CAN BE SAID that everyone has his or her own idea of what is right or wrong when it comes to temptation.

The weight-watcher who is trying to stay away from pecan pie watches someone else gobbling pecan pie and says, "You are yielding to temptation." In other words, "You are out of line." Why? Because in her own view, she is abstaining from pecan pie and she thinks everyone else should do the same. In her misery she wants everyone else to be miserable over pecan pie so that pecan pies will disappear from the face of the earth. She is, in effect, codifying pecan pie as a sin, because by so doing she hopes the temptation she feels over it will disappear.

A man who has never smoked has no idea of what a man who has smoked all his life feels when he gives it up as a Christian. But when that Christian should slip and light one up, the nonsmoker immediately says, "Don't you know your body is the temple of the Holy Spirit?" True. But for the nonsmoker who never tasted nicotine, it is easy to bring up the law and make the other feel guilty under the rationale of "responsibility to the other."

THE CODIFIED LIFE

Far too often people will set up a codified level of life on what they like or don't like, what they can have or are forbidden to have. They will then use these codes as a proper "Biblical norm" for all to follow. The smoker was wrong in that his smoking habit was damaging his health and shortening the life God gave him. But the approach to him on the point of the breach of spiritual law only adds new dimensions of guilt that often increase his anxiety and thus increase his smoking. Excessive morality communicates the wrong signals. The smoker needs love and understanding from the nonsmoker if he is to face his problem and win over it.

When it comes to a broad range of eating and drinking, the same hard rule seems to prevail. It is a fact that overindulgence in alcohol, for instance, can be destructive. The same can be said for overindulgence in desserts. The individual who is 30 pounds overweight is as much guilty as the one who indulges in excessive alcohol. Both should see themselves before God and *judge themselves* accordingly.

One man who liked to eat fish liver was castigated by another who said, "How can you eat that stuff? It's gross. God never intended anyone to eat the livers of fish."

To which the man replied, "How can you eat sauerkraut? It's the least nourishing and the bulkiest of junk for the digestive tract. If God intended man to eat grass, he would have put us out to pasture long ago!"

And so it goes. Absurd? Yes. When an individual judges others, or sets up codes of judgment out of personal likes or dislikes, something is being seriously violated in the love relationship that should characterize all Christians.

"But food will not commend us to God," Paul says. "We are neither the worse if we do not eat, nor the better if we do eat" (1 Corinthians 8:8 NASB). There is the warning that follows, of course: "Take heed lest this liberty of yours somehow become a stumbling block to the weak" (1 Corinthians 8:9 NASB). The point is that a moral view is not a legalistic view as such, but considers the highest good of the other person. That not only means taking heed of weaker Christians, but also not judging another for something that may not appear exactly right, and in that judgment hurting and adding guilt that may not be there.

GOD IS NOT PROVINCIAL

As one travels across the world, the impossibility of determining a universal law of behavior, if not morality, is seen to be hopeless—certainly in terms of interpretation of it, in any case. American Christians in their own sense of behavioral code run up against Europeans, Africans, and Asians in the same area, yet they all hold to the character of God as predominant. There is an unholy fear in admitting this, because it seems that the American Biblical point of view is not that universal; therefore, the conclusion is that something is wrong with the American view. God is not American, European, African, or Asian—nor is He Baptist, Presbyterian, Episcopal, or whatever.

God will not be tied to living up to any one culture's (or church's) interpretation of Himself in terms of behavior or lifestyles. His will is to set all men free from the bondage of sin and to be free in Him in matters of conscience.

Man looks upon the outward appearance but not into the heart. Jesus said, "Not what enters into the mouth defiles the man, but what proceeds out of the mouth, this defiles the man" (Matthew 15:11 NASB).

And as Ahlem adds, "One of the most acceptable ways of resisting love is to become excessively moral. You can become so upright, clean and dignified that you will earn barrels of social approval . . .; your image will be impeccable. Successfully comparing your virtues to the qualities of others, you will convince yourself that God will have to accept you. Certainly all this goodness will establish a relationship with Him . . . but if being moral is an essentially defensive activity, not a symptom of healthy growth, it will build a barrier between you and the needs of others . . . ."[1]

Is morality wrong, then? No, of course not. It is the *imposing* of a level of morality, personally interpreted level, that is wrong. The continual listing of sins out of a personal matrix of likes and dislikes, seeking some proof text to back it up, is the height of Pharisaism. For what does one do with the verse, "He that is weak in the faith receive, but not with doubtful disputation" (Romans 14:1)? The new American Standard Bible reads, "Now accept the one who is weak in faith, but not for the purpose of passing judgment on his opinions."

How can one accept someone weak in the faith if his personal code does not allow for acceptance? Something is being seriously violated in the love relationship that should characterize Christians.

Morality ought to be motivated by the character of God springing up within the soul, and not by something superimposed in terms of personal preference. It is character, not preachment. It is love, not law.

Biblical Conviction

But then who *does* convict? Upon what basis does an individual make discernment about right or wrong? If it is not other people making the rules and interpreting them out of their own matrix of likes and dislikes from the Bible, who then sets the norm? Priests, prophets, or popes cannot in the final analysis codify what is God's province alone.

Jesus said of the Holy Spirit, "And He, when He comes, will convict the world concerning sin and righteousness and judgment . . . . But when He, the Spirit of truth, comes, He will guide you into all the truth; for He will not speak on His own initiative, but whatever He hears, He will speak; and He will disclose to you what is to come . . ." (John 16:8,13 NASB).

Is it enough to depend on the Holy Spirit within to do the convicting, without someone else acting as His interpreter? Is it possible that a believer can depend on God within to bring a sensitivity to what is right and wrong, if that verse is to be taken on its simple merits?

If that text be true, that God has sent His own Spirit to *convict* of "sin, righteousness, and judgment" (and who is to doubt Scripture?), then why do so many people worry about others doing that job? This is the spirit of 1 John 3:21,22, which says, "Beloved, if *our heart* does not condemn us, we have confidence before God; and whatever we ask we receive from Him, because we keep His commandments and do the things that are pleasing in His sight" (NASB).

WHO SHOULD BE THE JUDGE?

If it is a matter of the *heart* condemning or not condemning, then why the fear and guilt over someone else playing that role of judge?

In many cases it is a matter of one person thinking or presuming judgment of another. In that situation one must examine himself or herself to be sure it is coming from someone else and not from within. But where one believer knows that he is the target of another's imposition of his or her rules of Christian conduct, then it is time to resist that "spirit of judgment" and refuse to suffer any jolt of guilt as a result.

Does this negate legitimate concern for one who might inadvertently be creating contradiction by some level of personal lifestyle? No. There is a difference between a person's approach to another in love on a matter that is quite obviously in need of correction, versus a person who comes in terms of law. The love principle says, "You and I are brothers. My highest concern is for you. I am only concerned that what you are doing may be causing you some harm, or perhaps someone else. Because I want you to know the fullest in God, I refer this to you for your judgment and consideration." Anyone can take that in the spirit intended.

But when one comes as a "moralist," who holds the gavel on another and reads the law, there comes fear. Fear does not bring forth anything but more fear, or even resentment. Love, on the other hand, does not breed resentment even if the statement concerns something that may be a weakness in another person.

One person who was approached by another in love on this matter received the kind words and said, "You know, I never realized I was even doing it. But you are right. Thank you for helping me to see that."

The point here, however, is that every believer must know where he or she is in terms of the concern of God for him. Paul caught this sense of personal responsibility before God with regard to inner conviction when he said, "Who art thou that thou judgest another man's servant? To his own master he standeth or falleth. Yea, he shall be holden up, for God is able to make him stand. One man esteemeth one day above another; another esteemeth every day alike. *Let every man be fully persuaded in his own mind*" (Romans 14:4,5).

There is the positive side to Christian living. The negative side is fear of others, fear of the judgment of others. The positive side is that God emphasizes "righteousness [doing right], peace, and joy in the Holy Spirit". If there were more emphasis on these three attributes of the kingdom and less on the negative aspects of law, there would be far less joylessness among Christians. Certainly there would be far less breakdown over unnecessary guilt, and far less tension among peers.

THE HIDDEN DANGER

The hidden danger in leaning on other people's judgments of what is temptation or sin is that the individual soon becomes bound to seeking someone else's approval constantly. Or else that person may find in another person a substitute for God's own work and responsibility in dealing with legitimate personal guilt.

One college student took on the moral perspectives of an upperclassman who seemed to know all about the "right and wrong of just about everything". The high spiritual standards and moral conduct made him almost messianic. Unfortunately he used it to the extent that he had a whole dormitory floor looking to him as a kind of "father confessor," one who would actually expiate guilt and sin. It soon became apparent that when students discussed a certain lifestyle or behavior, they would automatically ask, "But what would J.R. say?"

People who fall into this trap of allowing another person to determine for them what is moral and what is not soon become tied to this type of image most of their lives. They make no decisions on their own. They are terrified to make any. And if they do, "the soul will run eagerly to its judge," as Plato put it. Either that person finds forgiveness somewhere in someone, or he or she will seek punishment. There must be forgiveness or punishment.

Self-Punishment

Self-punishment is the second danger when others are set up as moral custodians of a group, and even more so when an individual leans on someone else to make moral decisions for him.

One young college student who went a bit too far in her romantic relations with another—even though there was no sexual compromise—did not look to God for forgiveness. She was trained to look for someone else, a "God-figure" who would act as the "father confessor." Her parents were that way to her all her life. Then came a select friend of superior spiritual morality. But when she felt guilt over an embrace, a touch with a person of the opposite sex, she could not bring herself to confess that to anyone. The result was that she withdrew into a capsule of self-recrimination in hopes of expiating her own guilt. She lost her personality. She lost her aura of physical attractiveness. She became physically ill, then emotionally paranoid. Her collapse ultimately meant losing out on school for two years. In that time she finally found her way back to God, who could forgive and forget.

It took a long time for her to fully grasp and accept that great truth. Five years later she did, but five years of her life had been wasted by allowing someone else to determine her sin, be her expiator, and actually play God for her. The tragedy is that she spent those years seeking to punish herself for her "sin." She never had the training to understand whether it was "sin" or not, but more seriously, she had not been taught that "He is faithful and just to forgive us our sins and to cleanse us from all unrighteousness" (1 John 1:9). There need not be any other "mediator between God and man save Christ Jesus." Yet people go on setting up new "pseudomessiahs" every day to whom they look for spiritual custody of their lives.

If the Jim Jones disaster proved anyting, it is that whenever any individual, no matter how seemingly kind and good and correct and even God-like, assumes and receives a position of such immense authority, the people who follow will soon be inexorably shaped by that person. In the end, as in the Jim Jones situation, disaster can well be the result.

The words of O. Hobart Mowrer are fitting: "A man is never whole until he is 'open to the world.'

This is not to say that a person has to shout his sins from the housetops. Not at all. But he is not fully 'saved' in the sense of being out of danger until he is no longer afraid of having *anyone* know the truth about him".[2]

One must not allow one person to command the whole gamut of life, no matter how spiritual. That person may well confuse the issue and compound the guilt on the basis of his or her own sense of need or innate desire to wield spiritual power.

It was *Jesus* who said, "Wilt thou be made whole" (John 5:6). He alone has that power and willingness to put together any life that feels broken over sin or guilt. The refusal to turn to Him and to instead lean on others says that there is a basic disbelief still operating within. That person need only turn again to Him and renew that faith to come to know the compassion He has.

Yes, by all means, confide hurt to another person when the other does not seek to take the place of God in the exchange. Share with another in tears—in mourning, if necessary; but in the end, God alone is the final appeal, whether it be in the matter of temptation or sin or morality.

One can only live a life free of false guilt—the guilt others may inflict—by trusting the Spirit within. Others may counsel. but that counsel must inevitably lead to God Himself. When such counsel is given with love and understanding, and not condemnation, the trail must certainly lead to Him.

Yes, one can enjoy life and not feel the crush of false guilt or even legitimate guilt. One must know the difference. The Spirit has been sent to do just that. He is the final court of appeal, and He pounds no gavel.

chapter four

The "How-Did-I-Miss-the-Boat?" Trap

HARRY IS A welder. But a good welder. But he is still a welder. Nobody knows what a good welder Harry is, except Harry.

There comes that day when Harry, like so many others, views the parade of those who have become "accepted in the beloved," meaning to him that they are the cream of the crop in Christian culture.

On that day the missionary is put on a throne and figuratively bowed to as the personification of true destiny for the believer. Nobody intends that deliberately, but it comes across that way. The businessman sits and watches the "heroes of the faith" doted on, listened to, almost worshiped "for giving themselves to the call of God." But for Harry the welder the guilt begins to creep in. He has not made it.

He is not a missionary or a teacher or a preacher or the head of a Christian business. He is a welder. At that moment Harry begins to feel uneasy. A sense of false guilt is beginning to take hold. He looks at his hands still showing the grime from welding, the grime that won't come off with soap. He dresses decently enough, but somehow it doesn't quite come up to the image of "successful, dedicated Christian worker."

Harry gives to missions and to his church from his hard-earned welder's money, but that won't quite suffice for the inner uneasiness about not making it himself in some level of "Christian service." Secretaries, typists, shipping clerks, truck drivers—name them. Many sooner or later go through this "How-did-I-miss-the-boat?" trap.

The situation becomes compounded when Harry hears about the "spiritual gifts"—such things as "the word of wisdom; to another the word of knowledge . . . to another the gifts of healing . . . to another the working of miracles; to another prophecy; to another discernment of spirits; to another diverse kinds of tongues" (1 Corinthians 12:8-10). Or again, "And God hath set some in the church: first, apostles, secondarily prophets, thirdly teachers; after that miracles, then gifts of healings, helps, governments, diversities of tongues" (1 Corinthians 12:28).

Now Harry doesn't feel he fits any of those. *He is a welder.* He ties steel together with flame! Where does that fit into the accepted levels of proper Christian work?

Harry's Mistake

So Harry makes his first mistake. He feels anxiety and guilt about missing out. He becomes highly introspective, trying to figure out why he is only a welder and not someone of much higher distinction in the Body. The introspection will lead him to try to allay his guilt by overcompensating for it. He will fling himself into every church activity he can. This he hopes will do two things: one, make up for his missing "the call" earlier in life, and two, evoke proper self-punishment for missing it, thereby balancing things out with God. Many a man has gone to extremes in joining every board meeting and every possible activity in the church in hopes of gaining favor with God. Somehow the "books must be balanced." So Harry does his best. And within a year he is totally exhausted.

This can all be compounded by someone asking, "And Harry, what do you do?" How can he say he is a welder? Could he admit this in a group of teachers, missionaries, preachers, and Bible study leaders? Again, guilt.

He may now cover himself. "Well . . . I work in construction, or more like design work . . . ."

"Oh, What kind of design?"

"Well . . . I stitch pipe and rods together—"

"Of course! You're a metal sculptor!"

Harry isn't sure that is right, but it sounds good. At least it seems to impress everyone.

But when Harry goes home his wife says, "Harry, you are a welder. Why be ashamed of it? Metal sculptor, indeed!"

That doesn't help either. Now Harry has left a false impression. More anxiety, more guilt.

PERSON VERSUS PERSONAGE

What Harry has done is put on a mask, but not his welder's mask this time. He has become a "personage," as Paul Tournier says in his book *The Meaning of Persons.* Harry gave up his identity as a "person" to take on the "personage," which is a front to save himself from feeling anxious about not being "in" with the elite of Christian occupation.

Everyone has a "personage" or composite of who he or she is through life, environment, and expectation. As Tournier points out, the real person can get lost in the personage. The personage does his thing but hopes what comes out is acceptable. The person becomes lost behind it, and guilt may follow as the individual senses that he or she is not being honest.

"I cannot escape the danger," Tournier says, "of trying to show it when I have not got it, of covering up criticism and irritation under a mask of amiability, the discordance of which an intuitive person is quick to note. Is this then the price that has to be paid in every noble vocation? . . . The master must hide from his pupils the gaps in his knowledge. The barrister must show himself confident of success. The doctor would do grave harm to the morale of his patient were he to impart to him all his doubts about his diagnosis and prognosis . . . .

"If the eclipse of the person behind the personage has taken on a new intensity in modern times," he goes on, "that is due to the technical development of our civilization, the concentration of the masses and the increasing mechanization of life . . . . The person is the original creation, the personage is the automatic routine . . . ."[1]

What Harry did not understand is that "it is the calling that makes the person," including the welding. Instead he chose to be someone else, another person—to rise to the images he felt were proper ratifications of his Christian life. In doing that, he felt guilt, a false guilt.

It is difficult to blame anyone for this state of affairs. One could easily blame Harry and those like him who feel this way. But they are often left out, holding the bills that others run up in their "higher calling." But it comes down to Harry in the end. He will have to face himself as a true person, which means "Harry the welder" and not "Harry the metal sculptor." Perhaps he will simply have to back off trying to make up for it all by running the youth camp and driving the bus when it is only an attempt to compensate for what he is not.

It may well be that church organizations are creating their own measure of havoc by over-emphasizing one form of calling over another. True, we should grant a salute to those who travel 10,000 miles to minister to some far-off tribe in the name of the gospel! Let's salute the preachers and the teachers for giving their all.

But somewhere Harry the welder needs a sense of ratification too. Because he "works for a living" is a poor distinction to lay on him. Because "he makes money" at his living is also a cruel deevaluation. Perhaps no one outwardly says that. But it comes across all too often. There are the "called" and there are the "uncalled," and the "called" represent bona fide church work and service. The "uncalled" drive fire trucks and sell insurance and weld.

GROWING INTO GUILT

The same sense of uneasiness and guilt creeps over the young, who are expected to rise to levels of "proper Christian service" because "you are attending a Christian college." Parents must take some of the blame for this. The students whom this writer has worked with for 15 years have openly confessed their guilt at choosing a "secular" job contrary to their parents' expectations. The tragedy is that they say, "But, you see, I have not been called." This means, "I have no aspirations to be a missionary, teacher, preacher, or whatever in a Christian institution as such." This may also mean that they are opting out of being a true Christian servant as manager of computer services or chief accountant at Sears.

The more serious complication in this is that they do feel a sense of anxiety in not rising to that "higher call." They have not faced it with God; they are too overwhelmed by the reaction of their parents or peers to consider that all of life's work can be given to Him.

One can even sense many times on Christian campuses a certain kind of division between those who are "bound for the mission field or some Christian service" versus those who are not really sure. Those who are not sure seem to group to themselves. They take on a form of the renegade, or think they do. In it all and over it all hangs a pall of guilt about not "making it."

Some students will try the personage route. They will talk the language, take on postures of spirituality, and seek to maintain a lifestyle that will prove they are "model" students in the Christian sense. They rise to the expectations of the institution at the expense of their own true personhood. They are inwardly aware of this mask, but it is their only means of negotiating the environment.

Thank God that Christian education is beginning to sense that each man and woman student must find his or her own way in God regardless of the elitist groups that constitute the core of Christian service and even Christian culture. But the church and the institution must work much closer together in order to prevent the growing dichotomy that exists between "Harry the welder" and "Harry the missionary to the headhunters."

One man sensed this in his own son when he was 17 and contemplating a college. The man was a preacher. He naturally wished his son to follow in his footsteps. But because he was wise enough to know that laying this on him was forcing him into territory that God might not have for him, he said, "Roger, whatever college or career you choose is up to you. I know God will use you wherever you are."

This sounds simple, but at that moment, the father was bringing his son out from a tendency to rest on his personage into a sense of his real person. God finds it difficult to use the personage, but He uses the person with great effectiveness. When a person knows who he is and senses no need to cover for it, there is no need to play games.

But to be honest about all this is not easy. As John Powell said, "Most of us feel that others will not tolerate such emotional honesty in communication. We would rather defend our dishonesty on the grounds that it might hurt others; and, having rationalized our phoniness into mobility, we settle for superficial relationships."[2]

But "Harry the welder" has to find his way back. The guilt trip has to end. The student must stop measuring himself by his more-spiritual peers, those with the "high callings," and must recognize that he is unique and that in this uniqueness he is going to accomplish something for God that no one else can.

Grasping the Upper Echelons

And then there is the other tragedy: those who push themselves into the "upper echelon" in order to be accepted. These will drop their businesses in the secular world and work up a "call" to rationalize their taking on Christian work. This, they hope, will make them feel less anxious about "missing the boat." Students will put aside other career aspirations to be a missionary, convincing themselves that they are "called" to that. These people in the end become whirlwinds of unhappiness; they can't fit in because they were not supposed to be there in the first place.

This is the danger of creating emotional settings by which the very atmosphere forces an individual to shift from his personhood to a personage, to move from what he or she is and knows to be to a personage who will be acceptable. As Dolby says, "Emotions often can mislead because they are volatile, dependent upon physical and unconscious manipulations by ourselves and by others. It is easy to allow the emotions to overwhelm the rational processes, permitting a person to become victim of fickle whims."₃

The emotional highs of too many Christians bring them to the jargon of "I am having a mountaintop experience" or "I know I feel led by God to this or that place." Emotions have their place, because the gospel is emotional. But the danger for the individual is to use it to assuage guilt about not taking a certain course of action which is expected of him by others.

One can cite case upon case of people who have moved toward Christ in a highly charged emotional atmosphere. But many people are more concerned with doing what is expected of them than with acting out of sincere need. In this case the move is not to Christ but to the person controlling the emotional center of that meeting. When it is all over, that person feels even more confused—and worse yet, even more guilty.

HOME BUT NOT HAPPY

Housewives go through similar problems of this personage versus person. Wives who stay home because they feel it is Scriptural feel guilty because they are not more active in community and church affairs. Never mind that there are young children in the house who need constant attention. Somehow that gets lost in the anxiety she feels in not "doing her thing for the kingdom." Some feel guilty because they are not leading a Bible study once a week. Some sense anxiety because others seem more active in Christian ministries.

Housewives often try to compensate in one or two ways: go out and start a career (which is all right, of course, but often creates tension with the spouse if there is not mutual agreement), or else plunge up to their necks in the church social whirl until they find it impossible to maintain a proper sense of order at home.

The Christian community simply lays too much on its own people with regard to what constitutes Christian service. A mother who feels constrained to give her children love and care at home should not be made to feel less "in" because she does so. Again, it is not enough to take a businessman's offering in the collection plate and not recognize his value in doing just that. It is likewise wrong to conclude that "money makers" are not spiritually the same as those who have become mobile in the territories of church outreach. When a pastor singles out certain people to be recognized—the teachers, missionaries, preacher's kids, and missionary's kids—as those who constitute some kind of "upper echelon," he must recognize the others as well—the carpenters, plumbers, salesmen, and secretaries as springboards to an outside world.

Unless that occurs, there will be this "personage-versus-person" syndrome going on in too many lives. As Tournier puts it, "How many people there are who are one thing at home and something quite different outside! In their homes they have themselves waited on like Eastern potentates; outside they live lives of devotion to others. Authoritarian, tyrannical and argumentative at home; patient and conciliatory in the outside world. Silent and unapproachable at home; chatty and companionable outside . . . .

"So we are all afraid of reality," he says. "We pretend to know ourselves . . . . It is not only the picture other people have of us that we are afraid of having to revise, but also the picture that we ourselves have of other people . . . ."[4]

So "Harry the welder" and those like him must come to grips with it. They need not feel they have missed the boat.

For one thing, as Francois Mauriac put it, "No one can look at himself except down on his knees, in the sight of God."[5]

FINDING OURSELVES IN GOD

Harry has to get his eyes off the horizontal long enough to find himself in God, to find that God wants him as a welder as much as he does a man who is a missionary to the lost tribes in the Amazon. There is no need to feel guilt or anxiety about what occupation a man or woman holds as long as there is devotion to God to be the best in that occupation. As Paul said, "The Spirit itself beareth witness with our spirit that we are the children of God, and if children, then heirs; heirs of God and joint-heirs with Christ . . ." (Romans 8:16,17).

There is no discrimination with God about heirship based purely on what a man does for a career. It is in terms of what a man *is* in God that counts—whether missionary, preacher, welder, architect, salesman, or whatever.

To avoid guilt about "not doing more" for the cause, which often comes down inadvertently from other levels, one must concentrate on *being* for God and not simply *doing* for God.

This is the real cure for moving out from being a mere "personage" to opening up our true "person." It is amazing how people accept that kind of honesty. A welder need not live with trying to protect an image of a metal sculptor. And Harry did not need to feel shortchanged in being a welder in the first place. "God is no respecter of persons" (Acts

10:34). God does not discriminate on the basis of what a man or a woman does.

No Place for Guilt

Since that is the case, there is no place for guilt simply on the basis of not doing what someone else does. As Paul says, "In every nation he that feareth Him and worketh righteousness is accepted with Him" (Acts 10:35).

Let it stand there. Let every man and woman who owns Him as Lord stand with Him on that. And let no man or woman plant unnecessary guilt, deliberately or by default, concerning the will of God for another person. And let no man or woman take that unnecessary guilt in terms of those who are falsely classed as being "in the boat."

Strip the shackles of inferior being, and that person becomes a person. All false notes disappear. He or she is at last free—free from the guilt of "wrong callings" and free to make the best of what he or she has! Such people have to be the apple of God's eye.

chapter five

Failure

WHEN GEORGE came home one night and found that his wife had left him, his first sense of remorse centered on the word *failure*. For weeks he became more and more withdrawn, always reminding himself and everyone around him, including two of his older children, 16 and 18, that he did not do right by their mother.

A look into George's 22 years with his wife proved that he was a caring and understanding husband as well as a fine provider. "I don't know," George kept saying over and over, still confused. "Maybe if . . . ."

"Maybe if" what? What he was going to end that with was, "Maybe if I had done so-and-so, I would not have failed her."

What was he actually referring to? Not much of anything. In fact, George really didn't know where he could have failed, but somehow he *knew he had failed*.

"I Wasn't Good Enough"

It happens to wives in the same situation. Jane's husband left her after 16 years of marriage without so much as a note telling her why. "It's like he died," she said. "Or worse, like I did something to him that made him die."

Jane had not done anything to drive her husband out. Her psychologist tried to convince her of that. But in the spiritual sense she could not detach herself from her guilt. Somehow she felt she had failed God. As she put it, "I fell short somewhere, and maybe my prayer life wasn't strong enough." For her it was a long time trying to determine what *might have been,* or more specifically what she might have done. Maybe she was not a good sexual partner. She began to blame her Christian upbringing as the cause of that, a much-too-rigid morality in terms of sex. In it all, she was taking all the guilt for the failure. Why not her husband? After all, he had left, not she. But still that did not assuage her sense of failure and remorse. "I wasn't good enough," she finally confessed.

Sometimes a death of a loved one will land cruelly on the survivor or survivors. When a father lost his son in an auto accident, he said, "I should have worked more with him on his speeding. I let him go, peel rubber all the time. I should have stepped in and done something about it."

It goes on and on. The guilt of failing a loved one who dies is common. Those who survive always wish they had "done it differently."

Of course, it's good to let it all out. It's better to face the guilt of failure, even though false. Wives will complain, "I didn't get him to a doctor in time," or else, "I ignored his symptoms and figured it was just hypochondria again."

GUILT AT TWO LEVELS

Guilt for assumed failures comes on levels: One is spawned out of a personal relationship where one party feels he or she failed the other. The second is born out of a sense of failure in the job or a failure to attain the fullest potential for self.

Many people come to a time in their lives when they feel their contribution to life or to their job has fallen short. In fact, the longer they think about it the more they feel they have failed. Failure is in terms of attaining *something*. In American culture everybody has to have *something* of great worth to prove success—a big house, a big bank account, trips to Florida every year, two cars, all the kids in college or graduated.

Again, students feel failure when they cannot attain a high grade-point average. Education is, after all, making the dean's list. When one is in a community where people are always hitting the high marks, the sense of failure is even more acute. With this comes guilt. "I snuffed off," one student admitted. But checking back, his fellow students said it was the opposite. The student in question was the last to bed at night, staying with his homework until all hours in order "to make the grade." When he didn't after two years, he quit. He simply disappeared, never informing his parents or the school of his whereabouts. Years later he showed up at home, after five years of working on an oil rig in Texas. He said he "felt guilty in leaving school and leaving home." He wanted to try college again, but it took three years to work his guilt of failure out of his system.

Maybe the words of Theodore Roosevelt have some core of truth for this: "Far better is it to dare mighty things, to win glorious triumphs, even though checkered by failure, than to take rank with those poor spirits who neither enjoy much nor suffer much, because they live in the gray twilight that knows not victory nor defeat."

James Russell Lowell added, "Not failure, but low aim, is crime."[1]

But perhaps these words of wisdom do not ease the burden on people who feel failure or the guilt of it, for life offers the right to fail. But failure in itself is not disastrous, nor does it mean the end for anyone. Even if the above cases of the guilt of failure are wrong, the issue is that one must reckon that life is full of experiences that seem to hinder the road to success, whatever success is supposed to mean. But in every so-called "failure" something new is learned.

For those who feel responsible for divorces or even the death of someone close as being a failure on their part even though it is unnecessary personal punishment, there is a sense where the individual has taken upon himself or herself too much of the destiny of others. Perhaps everyone has to have his or her brief journey of feeling this sense of failure and guilt. Better to evaluate it and face it for what it is than to ignore it, rationalize it, or attempt to defend against it.

But to live in that aura of guilt year after year, the sense of having failed the other person, is to crush life totally.

My Brother's Keeper?

Christians have to be careful on just how far they are going to play the role in being "my brother's keeper." Of course, people suffering in various dimensions of failure need to share with others, to get it out. But there is a tendency on the part of too many to overprotect that person even if the intentions are good. Some even assume the failure of those close to them, even friends, as their own. This sense of "collective failure" only breeds more guilt.

When one woman in a local church committed suicide at the age of 43, everyone rushed to her husband and said, "It was my fault. I should have done more," or, "Maybe I should have taken more time with her . . . ." As it went on and on, the husband began to feel all of these things himself, more than he had already felt. Again, the intention was good, but it was now after the fact. The taking of guilt in terms of the other's "failure," whether it be deserved or not, can become a complicated guilt trip for all.

If there is to be any help given to one who already feels failure in losing a loved one, the best help is sympathy and understanding. It is not in the best interest to offer counsel that leads the individual to think beyond where he or she has already been.

Job's comforters spent a lot of time doing Job's thinking during his time of pain in his failure and accompanying guilt. What they managed to do was lay more incrimination on him than he needed or deserved. They may have thought they were doing him a service, but they were actually complicating Job's recovery with God.

"I should have had Frank over more," said one consoler to Jane about the loss of her husband through divorce.

"If I had only known he was feeling these things," said another.

"I knew I should have taken more interest in his workshop in the basement," offered another.

So Jane begins to take on more guilt that others inadvertently dropped on her.

When a professional loses his job after 15 years of faithful service, he is already demolished. It is hardly helping him to say, "Well, maybe that wasn't your bag anyway, Joe."

Or again, "You should have gotten out of that place long ago."

And, "Who needs them, Joe? Obviously they didn't think much of you or they would have thought twice before making such a stupid move!"

Joe begins to feel even worse. He now feels that he has missed the mark completely in that job and that company. The less said, the better. Let Joe find his way through his valley, as it were. Fellowship with him, yes. Understand how he feels, yes. Encourage him about the future, yes. But to continue to dwell on *his losing the job* builds a fixation of failure that he does not need.

THE SELF-IMAGE CRISIS

Parents can do the same thing to their children. The young who pass through into early college life, for instance, may not perform up to personal or family expectation, as noted earlier.

When Dennis got a D in math in his freshman year in college, his father criticized him for spending too much time "socializing on his floor at the expense of his studies." What the father didn't realize was that young men at this tender age need peer-group ratification. The social time was as important for Dennis as mathematics. The father may have been right in one sense, but he did not understand the self-image crisis his son was going through. Making grades was important to Dennis in one sense, but making it with his peers was just as important, if not even more important.

Criticism of a person who already feels failure only adds more guilt. As Tournier puts it, "All criticism is destructive. This is probably why we all have such fear of the judgment of men. As with every fear, we are dealing with a manifestation of the instinct of self-preservation. We defend ourselves against criticism with the same energy as we employ in defending ourselves against hunger, cold or wild beasts, for it is a mortal threat . . . ."₂

Dennis wilted under the criticism because he already felt bad enough about the grade, but also because he could not express why he socialized with his peers so often. The father needed to understand this need in his son. But because he did not and reacted off the top of his head, he heaped on Dennis a greater burden of guilt. The end result was that Dennis stuck to his books, but by the time of graduation he felt he had become totally alienated from his fellow students. Whether or not this was purely imagination, the point is that he *did feel it*. And it would take him a long time to unwind from the inner sense of being a non-social person.

Yes, of course, there is a positive side of entering into another's tragedy or sense of failure. The Body of Christ works to close the wounds of the other. Who hasn't appreciated that effort? However, the attempt to close the wounds too quickly or wrongly may create the opposite effect. Sometimes every person has to bleed a little on his own, cry on his own, mourn on his own. To attempt to help rationalize the sense of failure is only to prevent necessary healing in many cases.

It is the nature of man to want to succeed in interpersonal relationships, whether in marriage, or in friendship, or on the job. Success in these areas is measured in terms of happiness with self, contentment, and fulfillment. At the same time, the one who feels *legitimate guilt* over a failure in any of these areas may have to experience it to understand the level of personal human weakness. Sometimes God will let it happen in order to reconstruct that individual to be more effective. God does not deliberately design failure for His own. But when it does occur (and life is made up of mistakes and shortfalls, some of the person's own making), then God is at work to bring that person out to a new level of helpful experience.

MOSES THEN AND NOW

Moses tried to lead a revolt against the Jews in Egypt while in Pharoah's court. He killed an Egyptian, hoping to spark the flames of revolution. It was not God's way, so Moses failed at it. And God sent him off to the wilderness of Midian to think it over. It must have been painful for Moses to fall from the great empire of Pharaoh and end up herding cattle in the wilderness.

But God let him have 40 years to mull it over. And then He met Moses head-on at the burning bush. In that confrontation God told Moses he was ready now, properly "experienced" in failure, to take on a new commission. God took off the burden of Moses' sense of self-defeat and gave him another start in life.

That new start was to take Moses far beyond a mere "pocket-revolution" attempt in Egypt.

And God is still doing this with people today. It is up to the individual to make whatever journey is necessary to learn from mistakes as God would have him or her learn. The only "failure" God knows is when one of His own deliberately ignores the warning signs, runs through the red lights, and determines to do it his or her own way. Then comes legitimate guilt—hopefully—but only then. The people who punish themselves when they have not run the red lights are taking a burden not intended by God. But the tendency to self-incrimination for every mistake, even when the facts dictate otherwise, is a turning on oneself which is damaging both to the person and to God.

An individual can go a long way before it all falls down on him. Samson blew it completely in terms of what he was supposed to do for God. He failed by deliberate rebellion in the use of his God-given powers. He wound up blind and grinding grain in a Philistine mill. And yet in the midst of that darkness—even though he *knew* he was guilty of the failure—God used him for one more glorious moment. Some may argue that pulling down the pillars of the temple of Dagon is not so glorious, but it was Samson's prayer that he might glorify God in the strength God had given him. In that sense, God heard and allowed him that moment.

If God can take a Samson, who ran through all the warning lights, and give him another opportunity, what is He prepared to do for someone who tried to do right but feels guilt in that it did not come out right?

The point is that no one can decide just how another person should feel in this fragile moment of guilt over failure.

LEARNING OUR TRUE CALLING

Take the case of the missionary who failed in his first term in New Guinea after only two years and came home in defeat and with a sense of shame. Who gave him that feeling? Mostly those at home. (Thank God, a few sympathized.) To those at home he had missed the mark, though they did not say so directly. To fail as a missionary is the worst of failures. He knew it.

"My, was it so bad out there, Bill?" someone asked.

"What really went wrong, Bill?" which probably meant, "Where did you go wrong, Bill?"

"What are you going to do now, Bill?" which really means, "You missed the biggest calling of your life . . . . what's left?"

What people didn't say directly to Bill they said to each other. Bill actually found out early enough in his missionary career that he was not supposed to be there. He struggled two years to disprove that. It took a great act of courage on his part to finally admit it and to withdraw. His feeling of guilt in his "failure" was already there, though it was not necessary to feel it. It would be far worse to stay someplace knowing that it was not of God's choice, simply to preserve the image and avoid the suspicion of peers on the field and at home. Those who do that should feel far more guilt than Bill, who decided to regroup and seek God for the right place to serve. The fact that Bill succeeded in facing himself with God meant that he was far more mature than he thought.

For Bill it was a long year at home, a time of spiritual reevaluation and a desperate attempt to get over his sense of failure. The church as a Body had to allow him that. Instead, the church leadership tried to find new areas for him to work in, to let him know he was still under the "calling." The intention was good, but all it did was to make Bill feel even more guilty because so many people were desperate to keep him in the "will of God." They were communicating to Bill that he need not remain a "failure" any longer—there is always something else to do in the kingdom to make up for it. Sometimes the leadership will feel nervous with someone who "quits a calling too early," fearful that the "germ" may spread. So came the offers, the recommendation for a "new start." Actually, though, as John Powell put it, "No one else can decide how you are going to act . . . everyone must march to his own drums."[3].

Bill did not go back into Christian service. He went back to teaching public high school. God used him and blessed him there, and still is. But it takes a courageous person to face failure—real or not—and to push aside the pressures of others and "do his own thing." But that is the way God wants it, and man has no part in that decision.

THE WAY OUT

Everyone has the right to find his or her own way out of his sense of failure and guilt, whether real or not. Fellowship and sympathy with that one, yes . . .

but any attempt to *think for that person, cover for that person, offer solutions to that person* may only complicate what is already going on.

Take the mother of a small baby of two months. The mother woke up one morning to find the baby dead in the crib. She took the blame wrongfully. The baby died of that mysterious "crib death" that doctors are still baffled about. But that mother said, "I should have checked on her all night," or, "I did something wrong with her formula." She had done nothing wrong. But those who swarm around her reminding her that "crib deaths are common" or that "God knows all about it" are bringing complications into that woman's life. If God knew about it, why did He not prevent it? That does not make sense, so the woman feels more guilt in terms that it was her fault.

In all of this, Morris L. West, in *The Shoes of the Fisherman*, said, "It costs so much to be a full human being that there are very few who have the enlightenment or the courage to pay the price . . . . One has to abandon altogether the search for security and reach out to the risk of living with both arms. One has to embrace the world like a lover. One has to accept pain as a condition of existence. One has to court doubt and darkness as the cost of knowing. One needs a will stubborn in conflict, but apt always to total acceptance of every consequence of living and dying."[4].

Thank God for helpful, sympathizing friends in the Body! Who doesn't need solace and the identification of others with failure, real or unreal? But each person must negotiate his or her separate levels of human experience, whether a morbid sense of failure and guilt unnecessarily self-inflicted or even the real guilt of running through the warning lights.

Man Is Not the Judge

It comes down to the individual in the end. Who determines failure? Guilt? It is not man! Therefore it comes back to God. He alone knows the human heart above all others. He does not accept "failure" as man does. As a Father He looks upon His own as children; when one stumbles and falls, He picks him or her up, brushes off the dirt, and says, "You just didn't see the ditch there. Now go on, and watch for it next time." Nowhere does God judge human frailty or failure unless it is deliberately courted by a rebellious heart. In that case He is faithful to chastise, but only for correction.

"If ye endure chastening, God dealeth with you as with sons; for what son is he whom the father chasteneth not? . . . Now no chastening for the present seemeth to be joyous, but grievous; nevertheless afterward it yieldeth the peaceable fruit of righteousness unto them which are exercised thereby" (Hebrews 12:7,11).

But why do those who have done no wrong chasten themselves? Why take on that unnecessary burden? One must carefully examine his or her own heart in the matter. To continue to rethink, try to redo in the mind, take on the responsibility for failure as it seems to be is to cut oneself off from the healing of God. There must come a time in this false sense of failure when the soul rises in a sense of God's rightness and justice and mercy and says, "God, I have done no wrong! Give me peace to go on, free from this weight. Release me from the guilt which I have taken to myself, that which you have not given at all. And let me live again, as You would have me live!"

And God says, as He did to Israel, "Fear thou not, for I am with thee; be not dismayed, for I am thy God; I will strengthen thee, yea, I will help thee; yea, I will uphold thee with the right hand of my righteousness" (Isaiah 41:10).

LET GOD FREE YOU

The Pilgrim's Progress emphasizes the love and support and help that God gives to His own on life's journey. All the anxiety and fear and despair are met and taken care of.

Then why not allow Him to do it? Whether or not there is failure, God is still the same. He never neglects His own who sense their mistakes, their missing connections with what is right. There is no need to live life and feel guilty forever—not with God. He is on the side of His own!

Jane found that freedom.

George did.

Bill did.

The mother of the dead child did.

There is "healing in His wings." So let it be! When failure comes, take it to Him. When failure is not there, but seems to be, take it to Him. But let *no man* determine the deliverance or the cure. It is in God and in Him alone, for He is never quick to condemn. But He is always quick to forgive.

chapter six

The Taboo Trap

A YOUNG MAN wanted to follow Jesus. Right on. So Jesus tested him. "You know the commandments," He told the young man. "Do not commit adultery, do not kill, do not steal, do not bear false witness, do not defraud, honor thy father and thy mother."

The young man answered and said, "Master, all of these I have observed from my youth." Good. He had all the *religion* necessary to make it.

But Jesus sensed immediately that the man had missed the point, and the Bible says, "Then Jesus, beholding him, loved him, and said unto him, One thing thou lackest: Go thy way, sell whatsoever thou hast, and give to the poor, and thou shalt have treasure in heaven; and come, take up the cross and follow me" (Mark 10:21,22).

The young man made his choice. Keeping the law was a lot easier than giving up material things to follow Christ.

There are not very many people today who would make a different choice, even among the saintliest. It is easier to *do* the necessary things of keeping the law and respecting the taboos than in abandoning all of that and everything else in order to *be* someone in Christ.

Was Jesus "knocking" the commandments? No. What He was knocking was the idea that if we fulfill all the law and the commandments, we will somehow have arrived, that keeping the jot and tittle of the law is more important than accepting the love of Christ.

THE FEAR OF GUILT

The reasons for the moralistic codes and doing everything to live up to them is the same old problem—fear of guilt. People miss the point today as much as that young man did way back then. People still would rather hang out their piety shingle to prove their spirituality than the promise of the freedom shingle that Christ gave.

People are afraid of "freedom" even though Christ promised, "If the Son shall make you free, you shall be free indeed" (John 8:36). Well, what freedom, was He talking about? The same freedom that He wanted to give that young man who was obviously disenchanted with keeping all of the commandments but still had no cause worth living for. Freedom in Christ simply means less worrying about the law and guilt and more emphasis on life, forgiveness, and "loving thy neighbor as thyself." This is what opens a man up and loosens him up. Law and guilt tighten a man, making him forever obsessed with codes and taboos so that He never sees Christ through it all.

The problem with living by the codes and laws and taboos is that it is impossible not to break one sooner or later. The Pharisees were good at listing them all, from washing the hands to keeping the sabbath. But Jesus wound up finally calling them hypocrites (Matthew 23:13). And He showed them why in the verses following. They made the codes and the laws but broke them constantly. And in one place He put it straight to them: "Woe unto you, scribes and Pharisees, hypocrites! For ye pay tithes of mint and anise and cummin, and have omitted the weightier matters of the law—judgment, mercy, and faith; these ye ought to have done, and not to leave the other undone" (Matthew 23:23).

The Pharisees kept all the law and avoided all the taboos, but they had no positive freedom in any of it. In fact, in keeping that law they were putting themselves into further bondage.

They strained out a gnat (Matthew 23:24) but swallowed a camel. The whole point was that there was no way the Pharisees were going to get rid of their guilt by keeping that law or even trying to do so. The reason people cling to taboos and moralistic codes is that they hope that somehow by the keeping of them there will be no guilt. But there is no freedom in that. A man cannot arrive at peace with God by his own efforts. There is no code of law or taboo that will bring a man to the fullness of the knowledge of Christ. The Pharisees tried this to win their salvation, but the Lord told them bluntly it wouldn't work. It is done today for similar reasons; Christians hope it will somehow make them less guilty and more saintly.

How can one keep the "whole law"? As it was said in James, "For whosoever shall keep the whole law, and yet offend in one point, he is guilty of all" (James 2:10).

The Tension Factor

The believer who puts more emphasis on the keeping of the moral codes than on the love of Christ is in constant tension. It is impossible to keep it all, so guilt has to come sooner or later, because something will be violated in that list. The tension factor is obvious in too many people who practice this rule. They are severe people who seem drab, gray, and fearful. They are not relaxed. They forever seem to be pondering what is right or wrong, what to do and not to do. Non-Christians are nervous around them, because who wants to be with a person who is forever dodging and weaving to avoid being trapped into violating a taboo?

One man recalled the years when movies were banned as taboo to the church. Anybody caught near a movie house, let alone in it, was in deep trouble. A law had been violated. This man recalled that as a Christian artist and filmmaker he had to stay in touch with filmmaking as best he could if he was to do a decent job for God. "But I had to drive around that theater ten times to check cars, people, and license plates to make sure I didn't see anyone who might recognize me. When I went in I stood nervously in the lobby, trying to hide my face behind an extra large box of popcorn and an extra large Coke lest anyone see me. I was attracting considerable attention by others who assumed that I was a bit crackers in my actions. The whole thing was ridiculous. If anyone saw me from the local church, then they were as guilty as I. So why the foolish tension and guilt?"

That movie was called *Ben Hur*, a Christian classic in the final sense. And yet what suffering God's people go through in seeking to be free to do what they themselves know is perfectly fine with God in terms of their own conscience!

The movie thing is long gone now (to some), but other taboos continue. This is the tragedy that seems to grip the Body constantly—the emphasis placed so often on breaking taboos and codes that few people, if any, see the glorious sunshine of a victorious Christ, of whom Paul said, "The law of the spirit of life in Christ Jesus has made me free from the law of sin and death" (Romans 8:2).

THE FREEDOM OF CHRIST

One must never confuse a distinctive Christian lifestyle lived in the freedom of Christ with the law that is imposed. The believer living in the freedom of Christ rises to a life of quality on the basis of the love and life of Christ in Him. The moralist or "taboo-keeper" lives his life on the laws imposed on him. The believer living for the glory of God is not anxious about taboos; he is more anxious about communicating the love of Christ to mankind. He knows in doing this that He will do all things naturally and correctly from the divine life in Him; and if He misses, He knows that God is there to forgive and move him on. The "keeper of the taboos," however, is constantly worried about fitting every dimension of law. When he misses one, he goes into destructive guilt patterns that take months or years to untangle.

The man who lives in the love of Christ and is concerned with communicating that love is no less holy than the man who is more concerned with keeping the whole law in hope of escaping judgment. In fact, the latter is less holy, because he is pinning all his worth on his self-righteousness. The man free in Christ is pinning all his worth on the life, love, and forgiveness of a loving God.

The taboos of "don't touch this," "don't touch that," "don't look at this," and "don't look at that" are not positive levels of Christian living. They provoke guilt. Again, this does not mean that there aren't wrong things in life—tasteless things, wrong acts, wrong visuals, wrong television shows, wrong movies, wrong books. But the believer who is free is one who knows he can trust the Spirit of God in him to move his conscience about such matters. The one who is not free is trying to live up to it all by himself and is therefore carrying a raw conscience.

THE SERMON ON THE MOUNT

One area that seems impossible to face, in terms of a moral code, is the Sermon on the Mount. Matthew 5 is seldom the favorite subject for the Christian's daily devotions. It is tough reading. Worse yet, every person knows that it seems out of reach to actually fulfill it in daily conduct.

How is it possible to live up to "Whosoever looketh on a woman to lust after her hath committed adultery with her already in his heart" (Matthew 5:28)?

Or, "Whosoever shall smite thee on thy right cheek, turn to him the other also" (verse 39)?

And, "Love your enemies; bless them that curse you; do good to them that hate you, and pray for them that despitefully use you" (verse 44)?

And again "And if any man sue thee at the law and take away thy coat, let him have thy cloak also" (verse 40)?

Or, "Whosoever shall compel thee to go a mile, go with him two" (verse 41)?

Was Jesus serious? After calling down the Pharisees as hypocrites for trying to gain righteousness by the law, why then this law that seems to be even more extreme? Having been delivered from bondage from original sin and the guilt of it, is the Christian now to sink into deeper bondage by trying to live all this?

Note, however, that Jesus was keeping the Pharisees in mind when he spoke these words—those who felt that their own piety and self-righteousness in keeping the law would gain them favor with God. In Matthew 5:20 He said, "Except your righteousness shall exceed the righteousness of the scribes and the Pharisees, ye shall in no case enter into the kingdom in heaven."

Perhaps Jesus was aiming at these Pharisees when He spoke the Sermon on the Mount—those who thought they were perfect by keeping the law. So now He says in effect, "All right, if you think you can win your way into the kingdom by keeping the law, try this on for size!" In other words, Jesus was deliberately trying to show that if the law is the answer to salvation, then *it is impossible*.

In this is a lesson to those who are trying to do the same today, even in the church. For in all the keeping of the law, guilt is going to show up somewhere, for no one can keep the Sermon on the Mount perfectly or even nearly perfectly. This means that a Christian life lived solely by this code is going to fail. All moral absolutes that are bowed down to as the "keys to the kingdom" are tyrannical gods unto themselves. They demand but give nothing back.

Jesus did not give the Sermon on the Mount to make His own people more guilty or more miserable. "Be ye therefore perfect, even as your Father in heaven is perfect" (Matthew 5:48) is impossible for the saintliest on earth. Jesus knew that. But He was again taking a crack at the Pharisees and anyone else who thinks that perfection by the law is gaining one inch in spirituality. And He is also castigating those who would lay such laws on others, thereby breeding unhealthy and unnecessary guilt.

The Sermon on the Mount, however, is not law. It is *life*, the life of Christ. It is not law but *love*, the love of Christ. "The law of the spirit of life in Christ Jesus has made me free from the law of sin and death" (Romans 8:2) is the key here. The *law of life* is much different from the *law of death* that the Pharisees practiced.

LIVING THE SUPERNATURAL

One person looks at the Sermon on the Mount as *unnatural* and forces himself to live it in such a way that it looks *natural*. Balsa trees are not natural inside heated houses, and yet at Christmastime people cut them down and drag them in. Since the tree is not natural to the house, the family hangs tinsel and other decorations on it to try to make it look like part of the living room and natural to the inside environment. When it finally withers and begins to drop its needles, only then does the obvious emerge. That tree does not belong in that house, no matter how much is done to make it look natural.

To live the Sermon on the Mount is *unnatural*, and to try to make it look natural to a person only shows up as death in the end. Many believers do exactly that. And then they feel guilty in the attempt or the failure of trying. Outwardly they keep it all—or try—but slowly their lives bend under the guilt of constantly missing the demands of it. Then they wither and dry up and lose their joy and zest for life that Christ came to give. Guilt will kill them in the end.

However, the other believer says there is a way to live the Sermon *supernatural naturally*. The supernatural is God's gift and fits the believer naturally if he allows it to fit. But if the Sermon on the Mount is imposed from outside by some human authority, then it is total law, and there is no believer, even the holiest, who can live under that. But if it is supernatural life, then it is something God puts on and into the believer, not as constricting armor, but as a lifestyle that is the natural extension of the character of God.

If it is a *life principle*, the life of Christ, then the burden of guilt in missing it occasionally is not exacted. Jesus did not want a life lived in hate, selfishness, sexual exploitation, and revenge. The Sermon is first of all His attempt to provide a *guideline* for a believer to live within a natural level while serving by a supernatural enablement. If the believer slips on any of it unintentionally, the life principle of Christ, which is compassion and love and forgiveness, lifts him up again and sets him on his way. If the believer makes it law, all that's left in the failure is guilt, the court, and the gavel.

THE PRINCIPLE OF LOVE

Jesus is saying on the Sermon on the Mount that *love* is the undergirding principle of any believer's life in living out the character of God. It is the love of Christ within and then the believer's extension of that love to others.

Love says, "I am not interested in hating my brother to think murder, because the life of Christ just does not operate on that level (see Matthew 5:21). And love says again, "I will not use a woman sexually or view her only as sexual, but I shall see her as a total personality, a whole being" (see verse 28). Love says, "I will not go only one mile with a person, but I will go extra miles, because Christ did that for me, and His life and love are within me" (see verse 41). Or again, love says, "I don't see my persecutors as enemies but as people whom God loves despite their treatment of me personally" (see verse 44).

If the Sermon on the Mount is looked upon as *life* and *love*, there is freedom in relaxation in keeping of it. A loving, life-giving God knows the frame of the believer—some days there may be a missing of the mark. He is quick to forgive when asked. At the same time, knowing this, the believer's pleasure is to exhibit these life-giving qualitites toward others out of love for Christ, and *not* because it is the *law*. There is a vast difference!

If the Sermon is looked on as law, then man is back in bondage, because every waking hour he is conscious of making a slip, of failing the mark. His whole reason for existence as a Christian is tied *solely* to the taboos and codes of moral law. The "law of sin and death" dogs him every day.

THE EXTRA MILE

Take the case of Larry, who was an alcoholic. He had only one friend, a man named Ken. Ken was a Christian. Larry had a "spiritual experience" but then slipped back. Many nights Larry would call Ken after midnight "just to have someone to talk to." Ken listened, though it was sometimes a bit exasperating to go on so long at that hour. But on one occasion Larry asked Ken for 20 dollars to "help pay the rent." Ken knew it would probably go for drink. Ken pondered. Should he aid an alcoholic in his habit? He thought a moment and sensed that maybe he ought to consider it. "It was the toughest thing for me to do, putting that 20 dollars in that envelope to Larry," he said. "But then I thought, maybe he does need it to pay the rent. So I put in another 20 just in case."

What Ken did not know was that Larry had come to the end of himself. And that night while Ken pondered whether to send the money, Larry was thinking of suicide. When the envelope came, inside it was not simply 20 dollars, but 40! Larry sat on the steps and cried. Someone had cared far beyond what he had even asked! And he paid the rent. That act of going the extra mile brought Larry back to spiritual reality.

Ken went the extra mile, not out of law, but out of love.

No Salvation in Codes

The Sermon on the Mount is likewise Jesus' way of saying, "There is no way you can gain salvation or merit by keeping codes or avoiding taboos." As Tournier put it, "As you see, it is just the opposite of a moral code; it might more readily be likened to a Socratic dialogue about man's powerlessness to attain genuine virtue and thus to exculpate himself by impeccable conduct."[1] Tournier further adds the significant key: "By practicing the narrowest moralism, a man falls into a worse guilt, that of self-satisfaction and the repression of conscience. One may carefully 'strain at a gnat' and 'swallow the camel.' A man who seeks to cleanse himself of guilt becomes even more heavily burdened with it. Those whom God welcomes with open arms are not the virtuous, but the despised, not those who deny their guilt, but those who confess it; those who quake with remorse and impotence . . . ."

Moralism has returned," he adds, referring to those who try to keep the law, "and with it the breath of the Holy Spirit is stifled . . . . What was a spontaneous impulse, free and joyful obedience to God, responding to His wonderful grace, becomes constraint, legalistic obligation and fear of criticism; pathological dread of taboos reappears. Above all, people begin to pretend to be more virtuous than they are."[2]

No, to live a life that is glorifying to God and which brings happiness to a person, one must put aside the straining at codes and allow the Spirit within to guide. "The law of the Spirit of life in

Christ Jesus" is what it is all about. That "law of life" as noted is not burdensome; it does not breed guilt, real or false. A person may fail at fulfilling the perfection of God, but God does not condemn.

In all of this, even for the person striving to live Christ by law, "Jesus beholds him and loves him." Those who suffer under the continual guilt of not keeping the "whole law" or even part need not wither and die. God is always there, loving and forgiving.

Yes, there is a principle of life and conduct that God wants from His own. But it is not a yoke that is chafing, a demand that is burdensome. It is a life that comes naturally through the supernatural within. When the believer relaxes in the love of Christ, when he seeks to make his life count for goodness, "to love his neighbor as himself," the character of God emerges.

RELAXATION FROM GUILT

Those who regard the Scriptures as a statement of indictment have missed the point of His life and love. Out of that comes only death. But those who rise to the beauty and splendor of the Son of God within them seldom struggle with taboo traps, whatever they may be as declared by man. Yet their lives are models of the true Christian spirit: The wayward and lost are drawn to them; the helpless and bound seek them out. From them come "rivers of living water." Their lives are not lived under the tyrannical fear of the commandments, but exude the trusting faith of a child who knows that regardless of mistakes along the way, the Father is there to lovingly heal and restore.

As Lloyd Ahlem put it, "Agape love, the unmerited, unconditional favor of God for man . . . we achieve our adequacy through this unceasing love. We do not *become* sufficient, approved, or adequate; rather we are *declared to be* such! When we believe this, we become achievers and humanitarians as an effect, a by-product of our newfound selves."[3]

There are many believers, despite good intentions, who need to be delivered from the bondage of the law. They need to be sprung loose to live the supernatural life naturally, to know relaxation from guilt and then to make their lives count for the lifting of those still caught in their perpetual cycles of guilt through lostness. The delivered person does not think about these words or the fear of them; he suddenly senses that the life and love of Christ are always there. And from within comes the true character of God—not something imposed from the outside, but something that flows from the wealth of God within.

Very often Christians are afraid of this approach because it seems to be breed a lack of responsibility for a proper morality grounded in Scripture, or perhaps because it spawns moral relativism. No! The Christian knows the lifestyle God expects, and out of his love for Christ he seeks to follow what Christ exemplified as true life and true love. But when one sees this morality, not in fear but in terms of the provision of God for spiritual health and fulfillment, and sees that Christ is quick to forgive, when asked, after a mistake is made, it then becomes more of a relaxed way of life and not a

restraining form of live. The pressure of account-
ability to God for every thought, and even for
actions that are not intended, can create a level of
life that becomes intolerable. God wants His own
to know joy, love, and freedom, even as He pro-
vides the internal resources to rise to a level of
behavior that is becoming to His own character.

THE WONDER OF GOD IN CHRIST

If the believer can move away from the heavy
sense of the judgmental sense of living, he can then
know how to avoid judging others. Nothing breeds
guilt more than emphasizing law over grace.

Archibald MacLeish had it right when he said:

A poem should not mean
But be.[4]

A Christian should not have to mean something
especially in terms of being the custodian of the
law; rather, a Christian should *be* someone who
has caught the wonder of God in Christ. That can
only happen when the strain of trying to live up to
all of the man-made taboos—the emphasis is on
mandate—and law is put aside. Know the difference
between what is of God and what is of man. Where
there is a sense of breach of God's expectation, settle it with Him! Then go on and ask Him to live out
His life and love within to the glory of Himself and
the lifting of others.

chapter seven

The Time Trap

THOREAU SAID, "I went to the woods because I wished to live deliberately, to front only the essential facts of life, and see if I could not learn what it had to teach, and not, when I came to die, discover that I had not lived.",

Few people go to the woods. They don't "have the time." Christians are among these, sometimes more so than those outside the faith. Time is a tyrant to many Christians, a taskmaster that demands 24-hour days or more for the sake of the kingdom.

People feel guilty about time and how they use it. It is peculiar that the Christian who has been set free to discover the wonder of God in all the universe should deny himself or herself that glorious experience by feeling guilty in taking the time to do so.

BURNING OUT FOR GOD?

When Clark landed in the hospital with a serious cardiac problem at 36 years of age, he had already burned through two lifespans in those short years in terms of work time. He was a leading figure in Christian education, a preacher, and a nationally known speaker on spiritual life. He served on five boards, was the lay preacher of his church, and wrote articles and books extensively.

When he had time to think about it all as he hung between life and death, he had to admit, "Where did it all go—and so quickly?"

Finally, after months of recovering, Clark realized he had fallen victim to the Christian time trap. From his earliest recollection his father was a man of immense compulsion, a traveling evangelist who would drive himself for as much as three months on the road. "God does not honor time-wasters," his father had told him flatly. "There is only so much time to fulfill His will, and any man who is not always on the line for God, making every waking hour count for the kingdom, is derelict."

Clark was conditioned early in life to keep pressing for God, as if "burning out for God" was a means of attaining greater spiritual stature. On top of that, of course, was the inner conscience that simply would not allow him to rest awhile.

"For me an hour sitting was an hour wasted," he confessed months later. "Sometimes I would even leave my company after dinner and go into the study to work on a new book or article or speech. I felt a compulsion to make every minute count for God."

THE EXTREMES AND THE MIDDLE

There are two types of people within the Body of Christ with regard to time. There are those who are quite content to do nothing, opting out for a relaxed and easy journey through life, leaving the causes to others. These may not get sick as early or have breakdowns, but they also have less to show for their lives.

The other is a compulsive worker, the "pseudomessiah" type, who must forever be at it to avoid inner guilt feelings. These won't admit to guilt, but would rather be known as "achievers," dedicated Christians bound on fulfilling the will of God.

There must be a middle ground between those who allow others to do the work for them and those who take on the world all by themselves. The lethargic ones push more work on the already-overworked ones, and those who take on too much destroy themselves far too early.

At the same time, there are underlying reasons why Christian men and women drive themselves to breakdowns. As Thoreau said, they come to the end of life and find that they have not lived. One reason is the ego trip. In many cases a Christian man or woman is seeking to compensate for a sense of inferiority by driving for mileage and perfection. This is done under the guise of fulfilling a mandate of God, but in actuality it is often simply an attempt to assuage a sense of bad self-image. Somewhere in this person's childhood there was a history of judgment about not achieving enough. Poor records in school, a failure in athletics, or a sense of feeling unpopular and alone all lead that Christian person to try to make up for all of it.

Turning It All Loose

The ego-tripper often is not conscious that he or she is doing it to prove something, to be someone, to show once-and-for-all that he or she is not a loser. Compulsive time-and-work-consumers do so out of guilt for failing to achieve earlier in life.

Mary was a shy, withdrawn, plain girl throughout her early years in high school and college. Because of that, she had not known any great achievements and had no real friends of either sex. In college she drove herself night and day to prove herself superior in her field of medicine. She was bound to prove that she had something worthwhile to give, something by which to raise her own inner sense of worth. She became seriously ill in her early years of medical studies and had to drop out. This compounded her guilt problem. Now she sensed that she was really good for nothing. When she did return to college, she turned to a major in biochemistry, but she felt she had lost something in her life.

When she became a Christian, Mary suddenly turned it all loose. Redemption to her was now a means to prove herself as never before. And God is faithful in renewing every person in His regeneration process to give them purpose and the means to achieve. However, Mary decided she could now make up for the "lost time" and failure of the past by throwing herself into Christian work. Besides being a medical technician and researcher, where she spent ten hours a day, she sought more and more leadership activities within her own church. She was driven to get visibility, to alter the earlier childhood years of being "plain, hardly noticeable, and average in performance."

She was now bound within Christianity, where such devotion is recognized and admired, to appease her guilt feelings of earlier years—guilt in terms of a poor self-image and a failure to achieve. Mary became an overachiever; while she was admired and used because she seemed dedicated and she carried boundless energy, she was unaware of what she was doing to her own body. At the age of 34 she suffered from a bleeding ulcer, had continuous migraine headaches, and and found her work as a medical researcher slipping. Despite all this she kept pushing, unable to allow time for relaxation and refusing to allow time to rethink, reevaluate, and find herself in God.

At 38 Mary was confined to the hospital with complications of stomach ulcers, colitis, and total exhaustion. *Even in the hospital*, however, she was always on the phone, checking with her work, her church, and the committees. She continually went downhill, and when the emotional collapse occurred, she was pushed completely out of it.

It took Mary four years to recover and find herself. When she did, she emerged as a woman who had found peace. With it came a new sense of serenity and attractiveness she never had before. She married at 43 and had one child.

But Mary admits that overachievers, even for the sake of the kingdom, can very often be pushing themselves to build an ego as compensation for guilt because of a bad self-image.

THE PAIN FROM OTHERS

Beyond the ego, people feel bound in a time trap because of what others inflict on them. Preachers too often have a tendency (in their zeal to get their church members moving) to dwell too long on "teach us to number our days, that we may apply our hearts unto wisdom" (Psalm 90:12). That verse in itself is accurate, but it can be carried to a point where people will feel guilty about not "numbering" their days and their hours. Some go so far as to declare that God keeps books and a time card on everyone.

In some cases people become concerned as to just how God accounts for time. Some say God does not count the time in a man's life until he becomes a Christian; so then if that person is converted late in life, he becomes frantic to make up for lost time. But if God does that, then the 30 years that Jesus served His apprenticeship prior to His public ministry was wasted time. On the other hand, that 30-year span was His own time of preparation, as important in one sense as the actual ministry Jesus carried in those three years.

Abraham didn't begin his journey until he was 75 years of age, but in those years he learned much about the kind of spiritual person he should be to undertake that journey. Moses' time in Pharoah's court was not wasted, though he did not accomplish God's purposes specifically there. The 40 years he spent in Midian were not wasted either; there he learned to reevaluate himself (all of which was certainly a part of God's plan) and then to prepare for the time he would deliver the Jews from the Egyptians.

So if one is to believe that God is a timekeeper on these terms, he is bound to feel guilty. Where in all of that activity is the God-given time to relax, to rethink, to reevaluate? There is *none* if God is a very hard time keeper.

Sometimes the driver and overachiever can make other people feel guilty. Some people are gifted and can do more in the time they have. These are often looked upon as the norm for everybody else. And if someone cannot keep up with him or her, guilt sets in again.

Pigeons in the Park?

One man, who was used to taking his lunch hours alone in the park feeding the pigeons as "my time with God and creation," felt guilty in light of another man who used his lunch hour to hand out tracts in his office building. Even going home on the commuter train from the city, that same man was busy moving up and down the aisles with his "witness." The "pigeon man" suddenly felt guilty and took on the "eagle mentality." Gone went the quiet lunches in the park; gone went the relaxed reading on the train on the way home. Suddenly he was everywhere under the pressure of "work while it is day, for the night cometh" (John 9:4).

But the people who sensed something terribly wrong in the "pigeon man" were the non-Christians with whom he worked. Suddenly the quiet, gentle, easygoing man had become some kind of devastating whirlwind. His personality changed. He became more intense. His work suffered. He spent more time confronting people in his advertising firm with the gospel than he did at his desk. In the end he was called in to give account. It was only then that the "pigeon man" realized what he had done, and when he was told either to "get the job done or find something else" he knew that all that flurry for God had only alienated the people around him.

The time trap is very often triggered by others who make their own anxiety about the use of time the credo for everyone else. The "pigeon man" was much more effective in his own use of time than becoming "an eagle man." No matter what a person does in terms of time, it is not to be the dictate to another person.

In like manner, there are those who must push their time because the nature of their personalities is naturally that way. A man who came out of the hospital after open-heart surgery because of an aggressive, Type A personality decided to work with determination at becoming a Type B personality—a slow-moving, pondering, "get-it-done-when-you-feel-like-it" type. But within a year he was more ill than when he had gone into the hospital. Finally the doctor told him, "Don't feel guilty about being a compulsive Type A who must get things done. After all, history moves on the action people, so why change? Be yourself."

So that Type A went back to his Type A lifestyle, but now he learned that he could find balance; he could modify some of that heavy schedule and still get it done.

FULFILL YOUR OWN CALLING

No individual can take on another's concept of time or achievement, even for the kingdom. Full-time Christian workers who are at it eight hours a day in Christian work can make a Christian who works for General Motors feel guilty because his hours are with automobiles and not missions. The man in General Motors uses his time to do a job that he is gifted to do, and in the end his time will make the money to keep the missionary on the job. There is no credence in saying that the Christian worker's time is counting more for God than the man in General Motors.

And yet one can sense this in dinner meetings or socials. The focus of attention on "lasting achievement" is the person who is in "full-time Christian work." The church has allowed this aura to be cast too often, so it is not surprising that people who are effective in secular work as Christians quit their jobs and try to get into totally Christian activity. Many times, guilt has wrongly moved them to make impulsive moves in this direction. And the number of people who have done so and found total dissatisfaction is legion.

The same holds true for the housewife who spends her time trying to care for three young children and provide a home for her husband that has decency and order. Many a Christian housewife in this role has felt guilty when listening to another housewife who has put aside her domestic life for a career. In women's Bible studies one hears the women authors, for instance, who give glowing accounts of how their time is being used by God in reaching "masses of people for Christ." Many a housewife has gone home from those meetings feeling guilty about not doing much except maintaining a home with love and care. The result? Sooner or later that guilt will drive a wife and mother out into the career arena in order to compensate for a feeling of not using her time properly. The tragedies that have followed in the wake of that are all too clear.

TIME SHOULD BE ENJOYED

Time is to be used, but time is also to be enjoyed. It is strange that the church cannot set man free from the tyranny of time in achievement. Even on Sunday, which is supposed to be "a day of rest and gladness," one can sense a flurry of activity and people racing against time to get it all done during the few hours that a Sunday affords. One church had 12 activities a week, and some people were there every night doing one thing or another!

It seems that the churches which have a quiet spirit and a sense of the peace of God are those which keep activities to a minimum, relationships to a maximum. The "activity-centered" churches, which are *doing* things rather than trying to *be*, have less a feeling of that "holy quietness" which ought to be provided for the frazzled people who have had time shoved down their throats all week at the job. It is no surprise that the church that centers on friendship, fellowship, and value of the individual, and deliberately seeks to give "rest and gladness," draws people without much difficulty.

PRESERVING THE PAST?

The other problem with time, of course, is that some people feel they must preserve time in the way things were done long ago. Institutions are guilty most of all of shutting the movement of time out and keeping the historical dimensions in. Time stops for these people and institutions. God created the place one hundred years ago, and that's the way it will remain forever!

This pattern of guilt is tied to tradition. To "get with time," to change the program, is to negate the precious treasure of the "founding fathers." Some of it is tied to the founder who is long gone but whose presence remains, penetrating everything and everyone with the need to be faithful to the "faith once delivered unto the saints." That means "We do what *he* would have done; we operate in terms of our past." Even when the institution is losing out in effectiveness to the present needs of man, the guardians forever insist that to do otherwise would be to question the very foundations. These institutions then lose their best young minds, the best ideas, the sense of a stimulating and invigorating ministry that could have great impact on the *now*. Most of the time the preservation of the past is only a kind of fear of the awareness that time must go on. There is fear in change, there may come guilt in seeing the sacred order alter too drastically.

This fear and guilt is often handed down by the forefathers before they leave the scene. As one man at 80 said to his prodigy of 51: "Harry, keep the watchmen on the walls night and day. Keep this mission pure to its cause and its faith; never deter from it, and resist the temptation to take it on some other road. That is your charge."

And so it goes on from generation to generation, until the institution soon begins to die of tired blood. Activities never change, methods never change, products never change, the way of doing things never changes. What is there is a museum to someone else; somehow those within seem to feel that this is a sure way to prevent the awareness that time really does not have to be reckoned with. The institution becomes a sense of eternity on earth. And yet the pain of all this is that it decays like everything else. The only way it can withstand time is to catch up with it. Only then can it remain young, because the young who come in will carry it on to new dimensions of life and effectiveness.

No, the founding fathers should fulfill their time and leave it to those who come afterward, with no great challenge to lock in the place for time and eternity. Those who inherit must not feel guilty in altering the destiny of any institution in line with what is happening in the changes of ongoing time. No one should falsely maintain the idea that preserving time is a way of negating the ongoing of time. God is not the Author of stagnant pools when it comes to the progress of His history. Time is given to use; when one generation finishes what must be done, another steps on the stage and makes use of what is for the glory of God.

No matter if the guilt of time is because of an ego trip, of a poor self-image of the past, of seeking to overachieve in order to make up for little achievement of the past or for what others dictate in the way they use it—the guilt tied to it need not be. It *must* not be.

Dr. Theodore W. Anderson, late president of the Evangelical Covenant Church, once said, "I would live as though I had but one day; I would plan as if I had a thousand years."

TIME FOR WORK AND LEISURE

The Christian should realize that God gave time for work *and* for leisure. The Christian should not feel false guilt in terms of feeling "there is only one time to go around, so I'd better get it done as quickly as possible." He should know that God is working to accomplish His will in lives given to Him, and that He can very well do it Himself if He has to. Beyond that He works together with His own and "does exceeding abundantly above all that we ask or think (Esphesians 3:20). This means that He can cover the ground that the individual himself or herself cannot fully cover in the time allotted.

To see that total sweep of God in the eternal is not to get so locked up in the temporal levels of time now. To feel guilty about not doing enough may have its place if a person is not doing anything, but to feel guilty when one is already active and working to the extents of one's energies—and not beyond—is but to distrust the God who knows the beginning from the end.

To refuse to make time for simply sitting and studying the stars at night or the wonder of a rose by day is to deny that God has given anything to man but work. If God Himself could work six days and *rest* on the seventh, why does the Christian feel guilty in taking a few minutes now and then just to appreciate the presence of God?

On the one hand, redemption opens the door for the believer to engage in meaningful activity. And he should do that. But on the other hand, it does not mean a charge through life trying to prop up the pillars of the kingdom, as if God were too weak to do that Himself.

But it is far too often *guilt* that drives people to these extremes. And this is false guilt. The only legitimate guilt is that which belongs to those who are indolent. And even for that one God is always willing to forgive the sluggard if he but asks. But for those who want to be used, who want to move in a quiet spirit through the activities of a redemptive being, then the first step is to put aside the guilt about time and realize that it is a gift that everyone must use in different ways.

People and human relationships are more important than stacking up credits in terms of working hours. To cultivate human relationships in a meaningful way demands that the guilt about work and the tyranny of time be put aside. There is a proper place for repentance on the part of those who destroy their bodies and their spirits long before God ever intended by the wrong use of time born out of a false guilt.

TIME IS A GIFT OF GOD

Time is a gift from God. For some the line will extend to a full threescore and ten. For others it will be shorter, but when the end comes, the big question will not be "What did I *do* with it," but "Did I really *live* it?"

If guilt continues to dominate the believer and drive him or her to *doing* out of fear that "wood, hay, and stubble" will be burned up in the judgment, then life will not have been lived. It will simply have been squandered too quickly. God will have as much to say about that wrong stewardship of time at the judgment than He does about those who did nothing for the kingdom.

The best way to live life in terms of time and not feel guilty is to realize that Jesus said, "I have come to give you life, and that more abundantly," (John 10:10). He did not say, "I have come to give you life that you might work ten times harder."

To know time, whether a long span or a short one, is in terms of breathing the cool, crisp air of a crystal-clear autumn night; to know the laughter of friends and not simply the pondering levels of theological strategy and endless debate; to sit by the crackling flames of a fire on some long winter night unencumbered by the weight of a thousand demands of mankind; to run freely with the wind; to know the joy of tacking with the wind and not mind whether it is to fulfill some particular destiny or design.

To be free of the guilt of time comes only when one knows this God who has given time for *life and being*, and not simply for *doing*. To get that freedom, one must simply fall before God and confess all wrong motivations in driving oneself in doing things under the demands of time. Then one can rise again with the veil forever taken away and the wonder of God revealed at last. One must put aside the idea of trying to measure oneself in terms of activity and accomplishment against someone else.

RETURN TO THE PARK

What it means is a return to the park and feeding the pigeons at noon again; swinging in the hammock again; listening to a good concert; walking through the art gallery; watching a baseball game—and then simply lying down and letting the world go by for a day.

"Come aside and rest awhile," Jesus said to His own (Mark 6:31). But one can only rest as he or she gets a proper view of time and understands the priorities of it for one's life.

Thomas Mann said, "Hold fast the time! Guard it, watch over it, every hour, every minute! Unregarded it slips away like a lizard, smooth, slippery, faithless . . . . Hold every moment sacred. Give each clarity and meaning, each the weight of thine awareness, each its true and due fulfillment."[2]

chapter eight

The Still-Not-Married Trap

"WHEN ARE YOU going to find someone to settle down with?" An all-too
familiar question. Consider it as a good intention.
But to the single man or woman the question is
loaded and sets off a chain reaction of guilt within.

The need for human companionship, the desire
for a marriage relationship, is very strong in either a
man or a woman. That must be conceded by the
single person at the outset. To deny this under such
slogans as "I'm a careerist and have no time or
interest in marriage" is simply to declare a dishonesty. That leads to inner tension, anxiety, and even
guilt. The fact of "how to be single and still be
happy" has its point. But every person senses, even
in this so-called liberated society, that happiness in
marriage is still the ultimate in fulfillment.

THE PRESSURE OF BEING SINGLE

Single people in the church often feel the
pressure of this even more than their secular peers.
The secular individual has outlets readily at hand
and can, if he or she wishes, find many levels of
human relationships outside marriage. The Christian feels no reprieve in the same way, because of
the Christian value system and the Biblical base
that seeks to protect the individual from pro-
miscuous sexual affairs that only demean and create
new guilt. So the single Christian within the church
or the community of believers senses more and more
the frustration of not connecting with a meaningful,
ongoing human relationship intersexually.

"There are just so many men to go around," one single girl admitted, "and those that are left are not exactly the prize catch of the year."

Perhaps she is a bit too harsh on the men, but nevertheless it gives a hint to the internal levels of anxiety about whether there can be any permanent relationships found within the church. Apart from the fact that some women may set too high a standard (though better higher than lower), there is a problem among singles that goes deeper.

For one thing, the single senses that the church is a family-centered institution. The church looks to families on which to build, and will cultivate couples in all areas of the ministry. These, it appears, are the heart of the church.

"To remain single in this church makes me feel weird," a man of 34 confessed. "Everything here is geared to the family—the sermons and most of the activities. To be alone and single comes off almost as being out of the will of God."

Guilt can be laid on single people simply by placing them, deliberately or inadvertently, on a lower level of importance. Families mean incomes, incomes mean offerings, and families mean the perpetuation of the dynasties that provide a "revolving fund" of future church generations. The single, as one put it, "feels like a sandbag . . . we are carried for ballast maybe, but that's about it." The single, to the church, as some conclude, seem to be unstable, cut adrift, unable to assume the necessary responsible leadership that parents can. Though it is a myth, it comes through far too often.

MISFITS AFTER 30?

Some singles who get past 30 sense they are forever relegated to the ranks of something akin to misfits. Even if they honestly feel that being single is God's will for them, the aura that hangs over them by well-meaning people prevents them from feeling secure in their status. A single woman or a man will sense people maneuvering behind the scenes to match them up. Those invitations to dinner and "dessert at our house" often wind up as a deliberate manipulation to play the match game. It winds up as embarrassing to both the single man and the woman. And it adds to the guilt, because a single cannot come to terms with his or her singleness. There is a sense where people communicate the fact that it is not a natural state to be in.

Other women who pass 30, the "highwater mark," as some call it, feel that the only validation for their singlehood is to "give themselves to God" in some level of full-time Christian service. At least then the church will convey legitimacy on their status and will declare with some pride that they are "separated unto God for His service." As one woman put it, "They mean I am now *married* to God."

Far too many single women have gone this route. It does not mean they may not have had some pull to God's service, but some who have gone into missionary service, for instance, reflect on the possibility that they were desperate at times for the pressure to be eased on their singleness. Perhaps God was being merciful in leading them into this "monastic" environment. But many a single woman on the mission field has had cause to wonder about it. This "Joan of Arc" syndrome, as one missionary girl of 37 called it, "can creep up on you when the pressure gets too strong and you realize that trying to fit into the Christian community as a single, where there doesn't seem to be any man in sight, is very real." For many of these, it has been demolishing to realize that they have gone this way out of a sense of guilt. Having committed themselves to service, there is no way back for most of them.

Single men do not have it as easy as some think, either. To go beyond 30 as a single man seems to indicate that something is wrong in his sexuality. Traditionally men are aggressors. Not to "pursue" women means that the innerspring of male emotions has been "sprung." Of course, the people in the church are not conscious most of the time that they are communicating this. But many a single male over 30 gets just as panicky in not being married as a single woman. For him there is no way to become canonized as a priest to a life of celibacy. In this sense his single woman counterpart has the advantage. A male simply has to dog it, keep moving, try to ignore it, and hope he can get his act together before he hits 40. The suspicion about him, however, either by the church as a whole or by his parents, can push him eventually out of the circle of the church completely. "It just becomes too much to try to negotiate," one man of 36 admitted.

THE DANGER OF EXTREMES

The danger in all this, when singles feel this undercurrent of pressure about their singleness or their sense of devaluation to the church because of their status, will drive them to extremes.

One extreme is to find reprieve by courting non-Christians. One woman 29 years of age admitted, "When I dated a non-Christian, I felt for the first time that I was being treated as an intelligent human being. I found it impossible to cut that relationship because of the validation I received from him, not only for my brains but for my total being physically. I didn't criticize the Christian men for their inability to do that, and I still don't. It just so happened that I knew I could not drive myself or force myself to connect with a Christian male in my church when I didn't feel like a woman with any of them. I don't know whose fault that is, but I wound up marrying this non-Christian man. I felt I had found a person I could at least trust, love, and respect."

It went well for two years, but the inevitable tension of her spiritual values (where he had none) forced too many nasty confrontations. She fought it gamely for three more years, trying to keep it cool, but one day he just left. Now she has a greater sense of guilt. She couldn't "make it" inside the Christian community, and now she had failed on the outside. Today she works for an insurance company, does not get involved in her church, and is fighting each day to hold off the creeping bitterness she feels. This woman confesses that she was hounded too long by those good intentions of the married about that line, "When is a nice-looking gal like you going to settle down?" That became too much for her. She couldn't abide the continual pressure about her single status, that she was a bit odd, or that she had somehow missed the blessing of God because she was still single.

The other extreme is when some try the mixed racial marriage to try to assuage their anxiety. Some of these have worked. But marrying across racial lines can bring a level of guilt too. One girl confessed, "I feel the guilt at times of marrying Dave, who is a black. I was in a church that was very straight on these things. Color sin black, you know what I mean? To be in that church with Dave made me feel uneasy; it was as if I had sinned, ignored a command of God. Yet we had a great relationship. Finally all we could do was leave the church and find one of more liberal tendency, which proved to be far more tolerant in love. I cannot say that I am entirely happy to be out of the church I grew up in, but at least now Dave and I have a measure of peace we didn't have before. It shouldn't have happened over a mixed marriage, but it did."

Others who are under this pressure to strip themselves of their singlehood marry interracially and interculturally. They marry those of other nationalities in other countries. Some missionary girls have done this. And some of these marriages have worked. But these relationships are the most difficult to negotiate. The single woman must now leave her own American cultural value system to assume the other one. Some of these women openly confess, "I had a terrible adjustment to make in transferring to his country. Everything was changed—the values, the customs, everything. I just had to dig in with all my heart and try to make it work. But the years of carrying on that struggle made me old before my time." The false guilt of being single should not result in these tragedies. The guilt in being single should not be there at all.

Pressure on the Young

Even the young high-schooler feels the pinch of this. In his or her age group (and up) there is that sense of pressure to make it with somebody of the opposite sex. Parents sometimes are the pressuring point when that person gets into college. The more the parent reminds the son or daughter about getting with it about intersexual relations, the more tight that person becomes. On top of that, when a college student sees his fellow roommates dating regularly and he is not, the guilt pattern is aggravated. Everyone must have his or her own time to develop relationships with the opposite sex. The young know when it is time. Some need the time to mature, to be sure. But when they feel that pressure to "get with it" they do so, and the relationship may prove to be his or her undoing. So what if the son doesn't meet a gal until he's 27? Or 37? The same with the daughter, though women feel the tension a little more. But who is creating that tension? That is the question to be faced.

The tender ages of early college or high school can shape a person for a lifetime. Therefore it is all the more important to make sure they don't have to push it with the opposite sex. The church and the parents have to work together to assure young singles that there is plenty of time to be concerned about a life partner or a romance. And in this regard, the young must also be conditioned for rejection early in life in order to avoid total demolishment when it happens later. It is not unusual even in a Christian college to find either a young girl or young man trying to destroy herself or himself for lack of rising to the expectations which the institution seems to lay on them with regard to the opposite sex.

There is no condemnation in being single.

BITTERNESS IS NOT THE ANSWER

Regardless of the fact that God said, "It is not good for man to be alone" (Genesis 2:18), there are people who go through life single. And they don't appear to be wiped out over it. Maybe there aren't enough men to go around within the Christian culture anyway. Maybe there aren't enough men that some women would be attracted to, nor women that men would be attracted to.

Still, some women—and in some cases, men—have become bitter about the fact that God has not provided a mate for them. One has to sympathize with that person for feeling shortchanged when it comes to this valuable interpersonal relationship. Some have turned morbidly inward, searching and searching their lives to see if they had committed some sin that angered God in this respect. In so doing, some have lost their winsome personalities, have allowed themselves to go downhill physically, took on too much weight, and simply "let themselves go" because there didn't seem to be any hope for intersexual companionship.

Others in their bitterness have turned to lesbian or homosexual relationships, desperate to get some validation for sexual function, and to feel intimacy. But this only creates more guilt. Some women have even attempted to ignore their sense of sex by becoming truck drivers, welders, plumbers, or construction workers, often in an attempt to deny that they are women at all. Men, who find it a bit easier to cope with singleness in their careers under the guise that they are working deliberately to get high enough in a career before marrying, take on horrendous workloads to prove it. In other words, by doing this they can try to convey that they are "too busy for women."

There has to be a deliberate facing of the issue, and not these desperate attempts to assuage guilt by extremes and false rationalizations.

The church should become more aware that the single is just as important as the married in the Body of Christ. The church may argue that it does this. But when singles are crammed into a ten-by-ten room in the basement of the church, just off the furnace room, for Sunday school class, there is a tendency to sense that they don't count for much. The big classrooms go to the homebuilders, the young married, the old marrieds, etc. The singles? Shoved off to a bleak hole in the basement. Value can often be interpreted by that simple circumstance. Let the church heed the cry of the single—whether articulated or not—that they want to be recognized in their singleness even as others are recognized for their marriages and their families. Singles must not be given the impression that they are the lesser in the kingdom of God because they are single!

SINGLE AND HONEST

But the single person must be honest about being single. There is no point in tossing it off with, "Well, I'm not interested, I'm having too much fun being single," when actually they are hurting inside. There needs to be an awareness of inner need, but not that which forces panic or guilt about what others think. Most of the time it means telling someone straight out how one feels about being single. Some certainly have learned to cope with it. They do not have the problem. But for those who have not learned to cope, it is absolutely necessary to confess that need.

Dolby, in his *I, Too, Am Man,* says, "To tell another person of one's own failure, guilt, insecurities, lust and love may be as difficult a task as a person will ever have in his entire lifetime. It has been said that some people would rather die than be known.",

Known for what? Being single? No, that is obvious. But "known" in the sense that they are not happy with it, that they have needs, that they seek sexual companionship, that they want marriage, that they feel guilty, and that they have "weird" sensations in remaining single. Get it out. Why cover it all with a facade of complete resignation to it when the anxiety mounts day by day, month by month, year by year?

Many a single has come to feel that something is wrong with him or her when he or she cannot connect successfully in the marriage game. Some do not even date much. They have come to a place of fear about themselves, and then a fear about losing out on a date.

THE SATISFACTION OF HONESTY

One young woman stated, "Whenever I got a date I was antsy all the time for fear I'd do something wrong and alienate him. I was nervous from the first minute to the last. I fumbled in conversation. I was unsure of my ground in terms of what he was saying or asking. I didn't know whether I should let him touch me or if I should touch him. I didn't know if any touch would blow me out of the car or not. I was afraid, always afraid, that I didn't have it to keep the man coming back. The more I thought of it, the more nervous he got. So in the end he didn't come back."

And yet she finally decided she would put it straight to the next guy who even bothered. She was attractive and intelligent, and she took stock of herself and decided she had as much as any woman she had seen married, if not more. So once having straightened out out about herself, she geared up her nerve to lay it out with the man who asked her for a date.

So, as she put it, "I told him as best I could that I was 33 years old, an executive secretary, that I had no problem with money, that I could take care of myself, but also that I was nervous about myself and what I could give to him in friendship. I told him I didn't want anything from him, and I didn't want him to expect I was dying to give him anything. I told him I wasn't sure of myself, but if he was game to take all that into consideration, I thought we could have fun together."

The man thought it was the greatest opener he ever had on a date. The two of them hit it off right there. She did not marry him. They had a relationship for six months that was fulfilling and from which she learned much about herself. First, she had been honest with herself and with him. In doing so, she found that her honesty won his affection for her. Second, she learned that she was a desirable person to be around, that she could hold her own in any conversation, and that if she couldn't, she could say she "didn't know" and leave it at that. She found that she had a lot going for her that she didn't know before. She is 42 years old today and still not married. But she has had a number of close friendships with men. "One of these days," she says, "it will happen. But if it doesn't, then I can go on regardless. I will always yearn for that permanent thing, but right now I don't feel guilty about myself. I am as good and as bright and as attractive as any other woman—and I might even the have the edge on some. So?"

HONESTY TAKES COURAGE

Take the man who at 34 faced the same problems. He was an artist. He worked in art. He taught art. But because he was a bit effeminate, he felt that somehow he was put together wrong inside sexually. When he dated, he felt the same fear with a woman, not sure if he was coming off right. When he had fewer and fewer dates coming his way, he sank into despair of realizing that he could never attract a person of the opposite sex. He became morbidly guilty about himself, then became bitter that he should have been reared by his parents in such a way that he had this stigma on him.

Finally he decided to take the biggest risk of his life. To tell a man about himself would not do. He needed it straight from a woman. He had a fellow worker, a woman, who was still single at 30. He asked her, "Do you think I'm weird as a man?" The woman never blinked an eyelid.

"Well, Harold, *you* think you're weird," she said, "and it isn't long before you get everyone else believing you. Stop being so self-conscious. Stop being nervous about your glands, about whether or not you are a man, and relax with a woman. You feel guilt about who you are, and as long as you have it, it will come out with people, with a woman."

That man caught it right there. It took a lot of courage to put it out like that to a woman, even one whom he trusted and admired. But after he had done so and realized that there was not anything really wrong with him, that another woman had told him so, he appraised himself more accurately. Today that man is married and has three children.

HONESTY MEANS NOT PUSHING

Honesty. Why fight "who am I?" all the time about being single? Honesty means not pushing anything, not trying to be anything or anyone other than what one is. This honesty says, "I am single. I want to be married. I have sexual needs. I need to be loved. I can lower myself to get it if I want it badly enough, but since I don't want to lower myself, I accept what is."

As Dolby says, "The pressures from without may be fatal; they may destroy the possibility of self-discovery or personal honesty. They may press in till one gasps for air and pleads for mercy. I can hear the voices of the pressures from without— 'Have you changed?' 'We don't understand you.' 'You had better be more careful.' 'Don't be naive.' 'How could you say that and be truly Christian?' Often at this point people give up the task of self-discovery. These pressures are too great. We find ourselves inadequate to break through the walls of protection and provincialism. We have lost ourselves in all our complexity."[2]

In the final analysis it is not sinful to be single. It does not mean that there is some curse of God resting on the man or woman who doesn't find a mate. It does not mean that God doesn't care. No one can plumb the mystery of why some marry and some do not and come up with a neat answer, even in the economy of God.

But the issue is that honesty about oneself and not apology changes the individual's view of self and life as a whole. The "complexities" need not materialize. The pressures without may have all their voices, but they can be shut out. The individual stands on his or her own ground or not at all.

The singles who feel they are rejected constantly because they are not intelligent enough or attractive enough or don't have those Miss America smiles are simply miscalculating the measure of human relationships. The same is true of men who feel they are not sexually attractive enough or "macho" enough. Knowing oneself and being confident in what God has created in that self is what draws a man or woman together.

Yet everyone must make alteration where alteration is needed. The individual alone knows what must be worked on to bring out the true self. The defensive posture that throws up barricades to the expression of the true self is not the answer. The person who says, "Sorry, but that is the way I am; I was like this in the beginning, am now, and ever shall be" is using a handy motto and delusion to have around you if they want to grow up.₃

In other words, there is a trap of putting oneself down for the wrong reasons; and there is the trap of rationalizing oneself in a certain smug defensiveness when change may be needed in order to emerge as God intended. To evaluate honestly in this way can very often be the key to moving out and finding relationships that are meaningful.

ACCEPT YOURSELF

The acceptance of self and the acceptance of singlehood is the dual key to removing such guilt. It is not a case of saying, "Who needs guys?" or "Who needs gals?" Rather it is, "I'd like a guy, or I'd like a girl, but until he or she comes along, I am what I am." God in the end controls personal destiny.

There really are no "old maids." There are beautiful single women and men who remain beautiful in their acceptance of themselves and their lives as they live them. The most beautiful and gracious are older singles who have not given up on marriage but have learned not to fret about it or be guilty in "missing out" on it. But to arrive there, if it is so, one must avoid bitterness, cynicism, rationalizations, and defenses for openness and love of life and of people. Guilt cannot abide long in such a person who has found that control, and life can take on a measure of joy and satisfaction that can superabound.

There will always be mixed emotions about singlehood. But face them straight on. Everyone has them, even the most saintly. That's life. But if life is to mean anything, to have worth, it is not all tied up in whether or not one is married. Life is to see God in all the mixed emotions, to sense His presence in the days of loneliness as well as in the days when there is companionship. To some that is not palpable enough. But it can be. Because from it comes that measure of peace without which the person goes through a self-destruct syndrome.

God wants the best for His own. Singleness is not something to feel guilty about. It may just be the best thing that ever happened, because every individual is not the same. Accept it! As Samuel Johnson said, "Know thyself, be thyself, and then express thyself." Single or married, it makes no difference. In the end God will not cheat His own— the love, joy, peace, and satisfaction will be there.

As one woman missionary doctor in Africa, lovely at 40, single, said, "Maybe I would never have gotten into medicine, my first love, if I had fallen in love and married. I'm ready to put both together any time, but until then I still have my first love. I thank God for that every day."

So let it be!

chapter nine

The Parent-
Children Trap

NOW THERE IS a "runaway house for mothers and fathers," called the Parent Place, in Seattle. Parents there are told it is okay to go off on a vacation and leave their children with relatives and neighbors.

In a *Chicago Tribune* article Alan D. Hass wrote, "This Parent Center tells distressed mothers and fathers, 'Parents are people too. They have a right to be imperfect, to say "no" to their kids, to have privacy and a life of their own.' ",[1] He added in that article, "A California self-help group, Families Anonymous, with 122 local units nationwide, is advising parents not to blame themselves for the failings of their offspring . . . you don't owe them round-the-clock chauffeur service, singing lessons, summer camp, ski outfits, a trip to Europe . . . or even a college education."[2]

So has it come around? Is it possible that parents don't have to take on the guilt trips about not doing it *all* for their kids? This view has come from parent-focused centers around the country, staffed by professional counselors, psychologists, and social workers who offer instruction and emotional support to beleaguered parents. The key line came from a Family Anonymous spokesman who said, "Parents need to learn to put responsibility for actions where it belongs . . . on the youngster." Does this mean abandoning the youngster? "No," replies this FA mental-health worker. "It means being concerned but not consumed by the problem. You feel for the child, but you don't run down to the police station to make bail every time he messes up."

"We are beginning to see that parents have too often blamed themselves for the way their children behave," write Alexander Thomas and Stella Chess, psychiatrists and authors of *Your Child Is a Person*.[3]

THE CONCERN OF CHRISTIAN PARENTS

There is no question that Christian parents do spend a great deal of extra time worrying about their kids. Being concerned is fine. But what about the insistence on continually trying to live their lives for them? What about the worry when parents feel they have lost some level of communication with the child or the teenager? Christian parents somehow feel that more is at stake. There is that "image of our kids," the image that must conform to what the church or the Body seems to have spelled out as "acceptable."

What parent has not spent his or her life, sometimes over a period of 20 or more years, to make sure their kids "come through all right"? And who, after all those years, find they have become what someone has called "the battered parent" as a result? Think of the many nights that run to two o'clock and then four o'clock, when a son or daughter is still not home? Who hasn't walked the floors on those nights and visualized terrifying possibilities that might have happened to them? Death on the highway? So wait for the dreaded phone call? Picked up the police? So wait for the police to call?

Dr. Robert R. Howard, a Minneapolis internist, is credited with coining the phrase "battered parents." He says mothers and fathers suffer from "bruised egos, fractured psyches, flattened pocket-books, and guilt oozing from every orifice. It is time for parents to unite against such assaults. They have nothing to lose but their familial chains."

Again in the *Tribune* article, Sharon Stitt, who founded the Parent Place in Seattle, says, "Parents are afraid of their children not liking them. It reflects a driving force in the American character; we all want to be liked. Too often the result is that parents try to buy their children's affection by giving them everything they demand."[4]

But to counter this, all kids cannot be blamed because a parent insists on battering himself or herself unduly over a son's or daughter's progress in life. Parents often do these things to themselves, and the kids should not be put in the dock for so much of it. The young grow up faster these days, learn faster, mature faster, and seek independence faster. They should not be blamed for that. Parents take on guilt about their kids only because they feel they must carry their children through every phase of their growing-up years. That can smother a son or daughter, *prevent* growth, and slow the journey to adulthood.

The battered parents very often have inflicted that abuse on themselves through overprotection. It comes from a false guilt, a fear that if they do not protect, they may be failing that son or daughter. It is amazing in so many circumstances how well the young rise to develop their own journeys in life when the parent allows that to occur.

CHRISTIAN BALANCE

The issue in all of this is that of *balance*. On one hand, Christian parents want their children to arrive at independence, yet they are afraid of it in them as well. In another sense, they want them to be dependent, so that there will always be a closeness and love there. In some instances permissiveness is the rule in order not to alienate. In other instances repression is the rule in order not to allow a libertine attitude that says "anything goes."

Many a Christian parent has grown old overnight trying to reconcile both of these, feeling guilty about not doing enough on either end. On the one hand is the commandment to "honor thy father and thy mother" (Exodus 20:12). Children should consider that in love for their parents. But parents interpret this verse to mean "in by 12:00" or "tonight you study and no social time." When the son or daughter does not rise to that, parents get fretful and become suspicious that he or she may be going into a a stage of rebellion. But that may not be the case at all.

The problem is that parents are trying to be perfect human beings. In turn, they trust and pray that their children will respond and become perfect human beings. It doesn't work out so simply. In fact, it often breeds complications.

The Christian position encourages parents to find that middle ground between permissiveness and repression. Parents must be lifted out of their guilt traps about their children, to learn to enjoy each other, to live a little themselves. At the same time they must realize that children are moving quickly into adult decision-making, and they must be allowed to if they are to be respected by their peers.

BETRAYAL?

When Jim and Mary found that their unmarried daughter was pregnant at 19, they went into near-collapse. First shock, then rage. They had worked all their lives to make sure their children grew up to be "normal" and to be models of "proper Christian behavior." So now what? They froze. Their daughter had "betrayed" them.

As the mother said, "We stayed up night after night to deal with illness she had, to soothe her tears, to guide her in her education, to provide a nice home, to help her understand the values of life. What did we do wrong? Where have we failed?"

So they battered themselves over it. Now when they should be enjoying something of life, they were back in the wars surrounding their children. For these two parents it was a case of "train up a child in the way he should go, and when he is old he will not depart from it" (Proverbs 22:6). So what had they done wrong? This one did "depart."

Who went wrong? The parents? When parents assume the total responsibility for their children right up to the time they are married, there is bound to be a reckoning with one in the flock who will not *fit*. That is, he or she won't fit the image that the parents have tried to project. How many lives can two people live out in a given 20 years or so? If they try to live for three children, they are old

146

before they are 40. There are too many complexities in child development, child behavior, child preference, and the individual child's internal levels of dependence or independence to attempt to live those lives forever.

One pastor left his successful church ministry because "I could not absorb the shame and shock of my own son caught in the using of drugs." Why not absorb it? Why is the guilt about the failure of one in the family the mandate to put oneself in the bondage of guilt over it?

There is a great passage that Christians should catch in this and grab onto: "Who did sin, this man or his parents? Neither," said the Lord, "but that the works of God should be glorified in him" (John 9:2,3). Does that only apply to someone else's child? That is often the conclusion, but it is too simple.

"But you don't know what this means to us," the mother of the pregnant daughter argued. "This is the worst thing that could possibly happen. How is God going to be glorified in her?"

Parents want it all to come out as it says in the Bible. Parents expect a due return on the efforts and energies put in to raise up that child in the fear of God. So now there is only guilt.

"I honestly don't know what to do with him," one father confessed in helplessness and despair. "He doesn't seem to know what he wants. He just drifts. My other son is just the opposite. He's a graduate of UCLA in law and going great guns. But this one is still chasing around in grubby jeans, and I have a feeling he's smoking pot. To get him to church is a major effort."

THE PARENTS' EXTREMES

There are extremes that parents have toward their children. One is the attitude that says they can't wait for their kids to grow up and get out of the roost. This attitude is caught by the children early enough. It leaves a mark, a sense of alienation in them.

One girl who at 18 wandered off to go on her own stated, "I always felt we couldn't grow up and be gone fast enough. It kind of left a hole in me. I didn't want to grow up fast. I wanted to stay around them. But there always seemed to be a sense of urgency on their part that we three get through high school and college and be gone. Maybe it was right that we did. But I feel I never had a childhood of warmth or appreciation from my parents. I didn't want anything from them but love . . . ."

The other extreme is to try to hang onto them. Hanging on when a child does not want to be hung onto creates its own level of fracture. Parents of children who insist that they sit with them in church on Sunday show that they want to hang onto them. Yet youngsters in their teens don't want to be hung onto like that. They want to feel some independence. They sense the need to wheel it on their own. Adulthood comes fast in a society that has already communicated adulthood as early as age 10 or 12. But when the children express that they don't want to sit with their peers, parents kind of go into a panic and feel guilty that they have not done things right—"Otherwise why wouldn't they want to sit with us?"

Again, battered parents—battered by un-necessary concern and guilt.

The point to remember is that no child wants to be watched and worried over constantly.

When the son of well-to-do Christian parents decided he wanted to attend the Presbyterian church and not the Baptist (that was always the "family church"), there was a big confrontation about it. Immediately the parents went into shock. Presbyterian? That could only mean—well, who knew what? With only one child, they suddenly felt alone. They could not attend that Presbyterian church, of course. That would only be ratifying their son's departure from the Baptists. The issue was small. It so happened that the son found more meaning in the Presbyterian form of worship. There was no need for the parents to get uptight about it. He was not sinning, nor was he bolting the accepted denomination in heaven.

What Is the Best?

There are serious concerns, of course. Parents want the best for their children. That is fine and right in many ways. But the problem comes when they want to make sure what is "best." And that is where the rub begins.

Anxiety jumps a mother when she accidently stumbles on some private note in a daughter's or son's pocket. Those notes are the expression of in-ternal reflections about self, self-worth, and world view. It is necessary for them to get it down in order to self-evaluate and know themselves. Such notes are their privilege and theirs to keep. But even if the notes show expressions of fear and doubt, this does not mean they are taking on serious kinks in their emotional or spiritual health.

One daughter wrote on a piece of paper, which her mother stumbled on in her jeans when doing the laundry, "Sometimes I feel weird. I have sexual thoughts. Will God punish me for these?"

The mother became panic-stricken. Sexual thoughts maybe meant sexual experiences? She shared it with her husband. He, being a bit less panicky, simply said, "Well, they all have it. Didn't you? That is, they all keep diaries and write to themselves about themselves. Right?"

"But not *our* daughter!" the mother protested.

Why not? But now two parents go into the deeps, fearful of what is going to happen to the daughter. Nothing does. She grows up to be a very lovely, very composed, happily married young lady. But a whole year of sleep was lost by two parents who presumed the wrong things needlessly and took on unnecessary guilt.

Staffers at parent centers have warned not to deliberately look for those notes written by their children who are growing up. And even if it should occur accidently, it is wrong to make snap conclusions about them. It is a journey every child must make to adulthood. Whether expressed or kept inside, they must evaluate themselves and come to grips with the reality of life.

Of course, parents want to develop communication with their children. They want to know what is going on. They want communication. But very often, as children get older, they don't want to share their inner thoughts with their parents. They are not sure of their thoughts. They are not sure of the accuracy of them. They may even go to extremes to guard their thoughts. This blows the mind of parents. "What have we done wrong when he won't talk to us?" Nothing. He needs to search it out for himself or herself.

CONCERN WITHOUT TYRANNY

Let it be established immediately that concern by parents for children and their well-being is absolutely correct. There is nothing wrong in it. Children don't want an easy ride; they want to draw on parents for discipline and for guidance. The battered-parent syndrome has nothing to do with this. God has entrusted children to parents, to Christian parents, and to others as a stewardship, a treasure to be guarded. So if a parent is concerned about children, it is not wrong. *God help a country and the church when the parents are not concerned for their children. And God help the church if parents don't care!*

Second, there is no way possible to take on the lifestyles or decisions of any teenager who decides to go his or her own way. Parents can try to communicate their availability, but to push and shove and nag and preach is but to alienate them all the more. Somewhere parents must give their children over to God. *Trust Him!* For them! How much of their lives can the parent control or influence? After 17 years of age, not much. And the age is dropping fast, to 15!

This issue is this: If the parents have lived and taught all they know about what counts in terms of

Christ, there is no need to feel guilty if one of the flock goes wrong. *Sorry* of course! But certainly not total despair or even illness over this "shame."

There is no need to feel battered over one who may not fit the image.

Take those parents of the daughter who had become pregnant. They talked a long time about it. Finally they decided that what their daughter needed from them was not condemnation and alienation for her "wrong," but love. So when they faced their daughter again, they both said, "We love you, no matter what. You are still our own. Whatever you want us to do, we're ready to help. But stay with us. This is your home. We'll work things out."

That daughter was overwhelmed to tears. She hugged them both and tried to thank them. At that moment the lines of love had been connected, with perhaps greater meaning than ever before.

Some children don't go through the traumatic experiences. Sometimes they just want to be by themselves, to do their own thing. None of that means they are "guarding something" from their parents. So why become battered over them? Be available to them when they have need. But to push them, query them, demand from them—this is where fractures occur, and then guilt comes.

God knows about it! There is no need for parents to suffer such trauma that stems from preconceived ideas about the health of a child. From 16 on, it's time to give them their head, to do what can be done, to be available, and to communicate love in all circumstances.

LOVE ANYWAY!

Let it be said again that parents don't need to fret or feel guilty if one of their own has not measured up. Love anyway! *Every child must find his or her own way sooner or later.* It may seem that a particular child is not getting it together. Love anyway! But it is not necessary to lie awake nights worrying about what went wrong. It is not necessary to take on the judgment for failing him or her.

It is amazing that the ones who seem to be "out of it" suddenly snap back and become completely "in form." Some may not. But they know themselves. They know where they belong.

To enjoy life and not feel guilty over children means relaxing in the fact that they have received all that could be given in love. Everyone makes mistakes as parents. But children don't see them as mistakes. They go on finding their way, still knowing the love they had at home and never forgetting.

It's time to end those sleepless nights at two or four in the morning, worrying about the children. Yes, make sure they have received all that could be received in love and acceptance! Make sure there is as much communication as they will allow!

But having done all that, maybe the Parents Place idea is right. "It's time that we now have time for ourselves. Our children will find their way. We are here when they need us."

A loving God does take note of all of it. If parents can allow that to stand, then the fear and guilt need not remain.

chapter ten

The Healing
of Others

WHEN A MAN of great reputation was found to have stolen thousands of dollars from the bank where he worked, he was given reprieve by his boss but lost his job. His reputation as a banker and upstanding Christian businessman was gone. He and his wife simply stayed home, both of them broken, both of them crushed by guilt.

"Not once in that year," the man recalls, "did anyone in my church come to me and counsel with me. I was in my darkest hour, and I needed help, but I felt I had alienated my fellow believers."

Then one day a man who had known the banker, but was not connected with his church, came to see him. The man had worked under the banker in previous years. He had come, he said, "Because I know that God does not condemn you. You have condemned yourself, and that is enough. Now I have come to let you know that I have not lost respect for you because of one moment of weakness. God is bigger than that. I am here, hoping I can help you rebuild your life."

That saved the banker's life.

WHAT ARE WE AFRAID OF?

Why is there a drawing away from those who are publicly exposed for some sin? Why does the Christian have the tendency to feel tainted by another's fault? Why is it that there are certain "sins" which the church will deal with comfortably and others that the people simply do not want to associate with?

Could it be that there is a feeling of guilt in associating with someone who has committed some sin that everyone knows about? Is this not the same attitude of those two priests who passed the victim on the road from Jerusalem from Jericho, a man dying in a ditch, and passed by on the other side of the road?

A pastor was walking down the street of a city when a distraught woman member of his church ran up to him. "Pastor, you must go into that building over there!" she pleaded with tears. "My daughter is in that place. You must get her out!"

The pastor knew it was a house of prostitution. He hesitated. "Madam, if I am seen going into that place, I shall lose my pastorate. That is a case for the law, I am afraid."

Why? Who sets the boundaries for our ministering to others? Why is it that there is a point at which we will not go beyond, even if it means helping lift the burden of guilt on someone else?

This issue comes down to the fact that believers are too quick to judge. They see the "beam in the other's eye" but cannot see it in their own. The easiest thing to do is to convince oneself that somebody really stepped out of line and the best thing is to leave him or her alone. That is simply a cover for a lack of courage. It is surely not Biblical.

Few have anything to say to the victim of divorce. Few have anything to say to the person who has had some sexual sin laid on him or her, extramarital especially. Few want anything to do with an alcoholic. Few, very few, wish to enter the life of a homosexual and try to help him, even when the person confesses that what he is doing is not right. Is it only because of lack of skill in dealing with these "greater sins"? Or is it that in doing so the individual feels overwhelmed by it, and worse yet, that somehow these people are beyond the grace of God?

GUILT AND JUDGMENT?

Could it be that Christians fear to get involved with these more "public" and more "heinous" sins because of the guilt they feel themselves? Or is it because the spirit of judgment holds such strong sway that the level of compassion of God cannot get through?

A single woman, who had lost her confidence in ever marrying a Christian man, fell in love with a non-Christian. She married him. Six months later the man ran off and left her. The woman felt guilt and remorse. But no one in her own fellowship sought to counsel her, to give her assurance that she could pick up again in God and go on. Why not? Was it because in the backs of people's minds was the idea that judgment is being properly served?

These are all cases of people who *knew* they were guilty. Why then were they so crudely and cruelly ignored in their need?

What about the college girl who was gradually going through deeper levels of depression until she took to drinking to ease it? It was obvious to that college leadership that there was something wrong with the girl, but she was ignored. When she decided to take her life and failed, even then no one really entered into her life to ask why. The only answer was, "You have violated a sacred rule of this college—no one attempts suicide here. You have embarrassed us and the people of God." Fortunately one man on the faculty risked censure by spending long hours with the girl until he finally got her through to God.

Yes, embarrassment. That is part of the problem too. There are certain levels of sin that prove to be too embarrassing for the believer to deal with or become involved with.

For the sake of the institution, some people have been asked to leave rather than "pose further embarrassment." Yet there is always a problem of contradiction.

When one college student was caught drinking beer at a local establishment, he was asked to leave the school. When another student was found guilty of stealing a stereo from a roommate he was merely "censured" and restored. What was the difference? Was the drinking of beer worse than stealing?

It appeared that the beer-drinking was an embarrassment, one of those top-level sins that could not be accepted. Stealing was not quite there yet.

This level of contradiction in judgment is what creates confusion, to say nothing of the serious erosion of moral values, within the Body of Christ.

DEFENDING THE DESPISED

Tournier calls this the necessity of coming to the "defense of the despised." But few practice it. The "despised" are an embarrassment. They pose a contradiction to the body of faith. So ignore them? Sooner or later perhaps they'll find their own way, and there won't be any need to face them.

Now of course not all Christians take this position. Thank God for those brave souls who know no boundaries in terms of which sins are safe to deal with and which to ignore.

And it does take courage to defend the despised. It takes courage to identify with those caught in public sins—the sins that everyone knows about. It took courage for Jesus to face that woman taken in adultery, the worst of sins, which demanded that she be stoned. It took courage for Him to refuse to condemn her, but instead to forgive and restore her.

One hesitates to speculate on how many people have been lost to the church and even the faith by the failure of God's own to rush to the side of those demolished by public sin. And how does one explain why it is handled so cruelly at times?

THE GUILT HEAPERS

A young man and his girlfriend, both Christians, experienced premarital sex. They planned to be married in six months. Feeling guilty about it, they confessed their wrong together before God. They felt assurance in His forgiveness. But then they decided, remembering the church rule that governed their lives, to counsel with the pastor and share it with him. They did so. The pastor, feeling first uncomfortable and then in defense becoming judgmental, insisted they confess it to the the elders as well. It was a "procedural" thing in the church's form of government, built on the Scriptural mandate "Those who continue in sin, rebuke in the presence of all, so that the rest also may be fearful of sinning" (1 Timothy 5:20 NASB). But the key word is "continuing." These two had settled it and found forgiveness—it was not a case of continuing. Nevertheless, the law was the law.

Unskilled in church government and that Scriptural admonition, the two confessed to the elders. But from there the elders felt that the rule was that it should go to the church also, in public confession, thus fulfilling "before all."

So it was that the two stood before the entire church confessing their sin. One can understand in one sense the need by the elders and pastor to do this, but it is still hard to come by. These two young people, still sensitive in the faith, still young in their experience, lost something of the faith in that hour. The sense of guilt returned, mostly tied to shame in having to divulge the private sin, already forgiven, in a public arena. The fact that it took many years for them to find their way back to God after that is evidence enough that the "mandate" was not in order.

FORGIVE AS GOD FORGIVES

Instead, why didn't the pastor simply throw his arms around them and give them his blessing in the forgiveness they sought and already had found in Christ? Why didn't he fall back on 1 John 1:9, which is a more fitting mandate: "If we confess our sins, He is faithful and just to forgive us our sins and to cleanse us from all unrighteousness"? Why must admission of guilt be compounded by more guilt? Is that not, in a real sense, mocking the provision of Christ in His redemption and atonement and advocacy?

Yes, when someone has committed a public act which has endangered the Body, or when that person *continues* in it, perhaps then there is ground for public confession. But there must be careful discernment in all cases.

When Colossians 1:22 says that we are now holy and blameless in His sight, does that not cover a multitude of sins that are confessed?

Concerning this verse, Hal Lindsey in his book *The Guilt Trap* said, "Yes, in God's eyes we are already made perfect; not will be, but are."

He adds, "Experientially we may be quite imperfect, but acceptance in God's eyes is not on how we perform, but rather on the fact that we are *in* Christ and God accepts *Him* perfectly.", [1]

Jesus faced a prostitute named Mary and said, "Thy sins, which are many, are forgiven" (Luke 7:47). If His provision of forgiveness extended to the sinner, the nonbeliever, would not that same level apply to those who are in the family?

Or again, "A broken and contrite heart God will not despise" (Psalm 51:17). If God does not despise contrition on the part of His own who sin, why must the body of believers (in too many instances) refuse to accept it, and instead demand an "accounting"? Why is it easier to work with the dereliction of a non-Christian—the adulteress, the prostitute, the alcoholic, the robber, the ex-convict—and declare the efficacy of the blood of Christ and yet not make it available and conclusive for those within?

CONDEMNATION BITES BACK

Perhaps it is wise to examine again if the reason for not extending that provison is because of embarrassment, the embarrassment of having one "inside" stumbling when it is expected that he or she will not. Can it be that this poses a contradiction which the believer cannot handle or refuses to handle in love? Or is that by ignoring them the act of ignoring will be penalty enough?

Heaping more guilt on those who have already confessed guilt is asking for God's judgment in return. Why not instead rush to the side of that one who is crushed by a sense of remorse over sin and seek to heal instead of condemn?

There is the further danger for those who condemn people "caught" in sin, even those who have confessed it to God, that they may feel guilt later on in their own premature act of judgment. The church that insisted on that public confession from that young man and woman has had trouble growing since then, and trouble within in terms of feeling the blessing of God. That is why Jesus said, "Judge not . . ." (Matthew 7:1).

THE "GREATER AND LESSER" SINS

Very often it seems that certain types of sins carry greater judgment than others. Or else certain sins are categorized so as to make those who commit them unqualified for forgiveness. A man may cheat on his income tax, be found guilty, and be fined for it. Yet somehow it is easier—or so it seems—to forgive him, because it is a "cleaner type" of sin than a sexual one.

A person may lie and be caught in it, be confronted with it, admit it, and again it seems that restoration to the Body for him is much easier than for a person caught in some premarital or extramarital sexual sin.

Yet all violations of the righteousness and character of God are still violations, regardless of the degree which man puts on them. All must be confessed to God. And if so, then the ones who have confessed must be accepted back into the Body, not "with doubtful disputation," as Paul said, but with love and healing.

Forgiving the "worst of sinners" demonstrates to those outside what the love of Christ is all about. The greatest gesture to the public of what the love of God is all about is when the Body stands collectively beside one who is demolished by sin. *Any sin.*

The Result of Judgment

The by-product of judgment in seeking "justice" demolishes the guilty person so much that it is almost impossible for him or her to recover. He forever feels that every calamity that befalls him after that is the judgment of God, or "God getting even."

One can argue against all of this by stating that "tolerating sin in the camp" is condoning it and opening the door for others. Then why did Jesus forgive the woman taken in adultery? Why forgive a dying thief on the cross? Was He not afraid of opening the door to others to go ahead and sin? No, Jesus trusted the work of God in that life. A person confessing sin is not one to be judged and driven further into the destruction of guilt.

Yes, those who sin and defend themselves, who deny it or rationalize it, perhaps deserve that judgment. But even then one must be careful in dealing with these, lest in so judging by harshness they may be driven deeper into the night.

Why so quick to judge and not be merciful to those who are already aware of their sin? Perhaps because in everyone there is an innate desire to get even with those who step out of line? Sometimes it is definitely a "holier-than-thou" attitude, a Pharisaical posture that looks down on those who have slipped. Sometimes a level of anger resides within that refuses to accept the "upper-class sins." But regardless of the why, the hand of judgment is severe, and if man insists on inflicting guilt and punishment beyond that which Jesus demonstrated or Paul admonished, then that one should stand in fear and trembling of God's judgment.

As Hal Lindsey put it, "God will not let anyone discipline His children but Himself. He would do it in love because He has set Himself free to deal with us in grace. God, on the basis of His indwelling Spirit, whom He trusts and has put into the life of every believer, is conforming us daily into the image of Jesus."[2]

The whole point is that when the believer or the church does not move in love toward that one who has been demolished by sin, then that person is going to carry unresolved guilt forever. A man or woman may plead his or her cause before God and receive His promise, but many people must find ratification for that in the fellowship of believers. It is not a lack of faith on their part, but simply that some people need to know that it is all right with others in the faith as well. As Paul said in Romans 14:1, "Him that is weak in the faith receive, but not to doubtful disputations." Or as the New American Standard Bible puts it: "Now accept the one who is weak in faith, but not for the purpose of passing judgment on his opinions." The latter interpretation cautions about a double standard—to accept the weak one and yet judge at the same time. Paul adds in Romans 15:7, "Wherefore accept one another, just as Christ also accepted us to the glory of God" (NASB).

Unresolved guilt leads to destruction. If the church or the Body of Christians does not help the individual resolve that guilt, then the responsibility lies on those Christians. Then guilt becomes as much a part of them as of the guilty one whom they refused to forgive.

HEAL AND RESTORE

The responsibility is to heal, not condemn. Those who know their guilt must first be shown the richness of the compassion of Christ. "Therefore He is able also to save to the uttermost—completely, perfectly, finally and for all time and eternity—those who come to God through Him, since He is always living to make petition to God intercede with Him and intervene for them" (Hebrews 7:25, Amplified Bible). So the first step in healing for anyone demolished by conscious guilt and sin is to lead him or her to God Himself.

Second, the believer or the Body must restore that individual to the fellowship. As Paul put it in Galatians 6:1, "Brethren, even if a man is caught in any trespass, you who are spiritual *restore* such a one in a spirit of gentleness, looking to yourself, lest you too be tempted." And in verse 2, "Bear one another's burdens, and thus fulfill the law of Christ."

Restoring means giving confidence back, helping to rebuild the life. That man who went to the banker did that in just one sentence. That banker in a year found himself again, and once more he became employed by another bank because the president, who was a Christian, put out his hands to him in love and renewed him.

Then to clinch it, give that person *responsibility* in the handling of the matters of faith. A man or woman suffering through the pangs of failure and guilt must not only be received and restored but must also be given a sense of trust by his or her peers. This means deliberately putting their hands to work again in the cause of the kingdom. Some may say that is going too far. "How can a divorcee teach Sunday school?" some would argue. "How can one who stole be trusted to take up the offering?" says another.

Well, how is it that John Mark failed Paul and was dismissed by him, and yet Paul later said, "Bring Mark to me"? Paul was ready to forgive, receive, restore, and give responsibility back to Mark.

One pastor knew the cost of this and also the reward. A man came into his prayer meeting one night when he was finishing up on the text in Philemon, "And if he [Onesimus, the runaway slave] has wronged you in any way, or owes you anything, charge that to my account" (verse 18). That pastor admonished his people to "take a risk for someone, and let them charge their wrongs to your account."

That man who had come in went to see this pastor the next week. He confessed that he had just gotten out of prison for armed robbery. "I found Christ in jail, and asked His forgiveness," the man said. "Now I am out, but I can't find a job. However, the local bank has offered me a job bagging pennies, but only if I can get a reputable person to sign for my character."

The pastor cleared his throat uncomfortably. "Well . . ."

"I don't mean to embarrass you," the man said. "But I heard you say that people should take risks for others even if it means charging their wrongs to your account, correct?"

The pastor knew what he had to do. It was a case of either "put up or shut up." So with some trembling, but knowing he must, he signed the paper, committing himself for a man who had just gotten out of jail.

Yet that man went on from bagging pennies to become a top officer of the bank within five years. Today he is still in banking, and every year he sends a Christmas message to that pastor: "Thank you for risking yourself for me!"

That is what is meant by healing those who are suffering from past sins. What is true of the one who sinned as a non-Christian is as true for those who are in the faith. Risk-taking is necessary to help reconstruct a life demolished by sin and guilt.

Is this too much to ask? Only once does the saintliest and purist of all have to walk in the shoes of one demolished by sin to know how important all of this is. Is it not better to take on the attitude of Christ toward that woman taken in adultery: "Neither do I condemn thee"?

THE ROAD TO REAL PEACE

It is the responsibility of the one who has sinned to make it right with God. But it is the responsibility of those in the Body to receive that one into the fellowship in perfect trust and acceptance. To do otherwise is to negate God's provision in Christ. Only a sin-bound, lost person who has experienced redemption and the glory of release from guilt can know how important it is to always stand with one who is down by the crippling power of guilt. Any heart that freezes up toward another broken by sin has forgotten the glory of that moment.

If the world cannot see that happening within the Body, then Christ is veiled off from them.

There is no greater fulfillment in God than to reach out in healing to one who is suffering the ravages of guilt. They do not want rationalization or defense—they need genuine love and acceptance.

And in doing so, the person who forgives and accepts can likewise know what it means to enjoy life and not feel guilty. This is the ultimate expression of living.

Chapter Notes

Chapter 1—Will the Real Guilt Please Stand Up?

1. James R. Dolby, *I Too Am Man*, copyright © 1969, used by permission of Word Books Publishers, Waco, Texas, page 34.
2. John McKenzie, *Guilt: The Meaning and Significance* (Nashville, Tennessee: Abingdon Press, 1962), page 26.
3. Leslie Weatherhead, *Psychology, Religion and Healing* (New York, Abingdon Press, 1951, page 136).
4. Reprinted from *Why Am I Afraid to Tell You Who I Am?* by John Powell, © 1969, Argus Communications. Used with permission from Argus Communications, Niles, Illinois, page 20.
5. Ibid., page 11.
6. Paul Tournier, *Guilt and Grace* English translation copyright ©, 1962 by Hodder and Stoughton Ltd. Reprinted by permission of Harper and Row Publishers, Inc., page 17.

Chapter 2—The Guilt of Not Fitting In

1. Lloyd H. Ahlem, *Do I Have to Be Me? The Psychology of Human Need*, copyright ©, 1973, used by permission, Regal Books, Ventura, California, page 79. (Glendale, California: Regal Books, 1973), page 79.
2. Ibid., page 81.
3. Ibid., page 47.

Chapter 3—Who Judges?

1. Ahlem, op cit., page 29.
2. O. Herbert Mowrer, *The New Group Therapy* (Princeton, New Jersey: D. Van Nostrand Co., Inc., 1964).

Chapter 4—The "How-Did-I-Miss-the Boat?" Trap

1. Paul Tournier, *The Meaning of Persons* (London: SCM Press, 1966), page 38;39.
2. Powell, op. cit., page 89.
3. Dolby, op. cit., page 28.
4. Tournier, op. cit., page 53,152.
5. Francois Mauriac, *Journal*, Grasset, Paris.

Chapter 5—Failure

1. James Russell Lowell, *For an Autograph*, 1868, Stanza 5, Bartlett's Quotations (Little, Brown and Co., Boston, 1955) page 590.
2. Tournier, *Guilt and Grace*, Harper and Row, Publishers, New York, 1961) page 81.
3. Powell, op. cit., page 120.
4. Morris L. West, *The Shoes of the Fisherman* (Pocket Books, Div. of Simon and Schuster, New York, 1978)

Chapter 6—The Taboo Trap

1. Tournier, *Guilt and Grace* op. cit. page 122.
2. Tournier op. cit., pages 122,126.
3. Ahlem, op. cit., page 71.
4. Archibald McLeish, *Ars Poetical*, 1926 Bartlett's op. cit., page 960.

Chapter 7—The Time Trap

1. Thoreau, *Where I Live and What I Live For*, Bartlett's op. cit., page 590.
2. Thomas Mann, *The Beloved Returns*, (Knopf Press, 201 East 50th, New York, New York).

Chapter 8—The Still-Not-Married Trap

1. Dolby, op. cit., page 3.
2. Ibid., page 5.
3. Powell, op. cit., page 167.

Chapter 9—The Parent-Children Trap

1. From an article by Alan D. Hess, in *Chicago Tribune*, July 27, 1980, Section 12, Page 3.
2. Ibid.
3. Alexander Thomas and Stella Chase, *Your Child Is a Person*, (Viking-Compass, New York) ref. Chicago Tribune op. cit.
4. *Chicago Tribune*, op. cit.

Chapter 10—The Healing of Others

1. *The Guilt Trip*, from *The Guilt Trip* by Hal Lindsey, excerpted from *Satan Is Alive And Well On Planet Earth* by Hal Lindsey and C.C. Carlson, 1972 by the Zondervon Corp, page 10.
2. Ibid., page 24; 25.